HOUSE OF COMMONS   SESS

FOREIGN AFFAIRS
COMMITTEE

Third Report

THE EXPANDING RÔLE OF THE
UNITED NATIONS AND ITS IMPLICATIONS
FOR UNITED KINGDOM POLICY

VOLUME I

Report, together with the
Proceedings of the Committee

Ordered by The House of Commons *to be pi*
23 June 1993

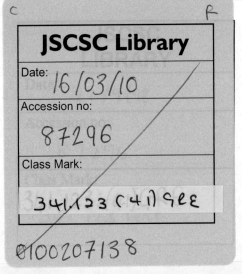

LONDON· HMSO

The Foreign Affairs Committee is appointed under SO No 130 to examine the expenditure administration and policy of the Foreign and Commonwealth Office and of associated public bodies.

The Committee consists of 11 members. It has a quorum of three. Unless the House otherwise orders, all Members nominated to the Committee continue to be members of it for the remainder of the Parliament.

The Committee has power:

(a) to send for persons, papers and records, to sit notwithstanding any adjournment of the House, to adjourn from place to place, and to report from time to time;

(b) to appoint specialist advisers either to supply information which is not readily available or to elucidate matters of complexity within the Committee's order of reference;

(c) to communicate to any other such committee its evidence and any other documents relating to matters of common interest; and

(d) to meet concurrently with any such other committee for the purpose of deliberating, taking evidence, or considering draft reports.

The Committee has power to appoint one sub-committee and to report from time to time the minutes of evidence taken before it. The sub-committee has power to send for persons, papers and records, to sit notwithstanding any adjournment of the House, and to adjourn from place to place. It has a quorum of three.

The membership of the Committee since its appointment on 13 July 1992 is as follows:

Rt Hon David Howell, *Guildford* (Chairman)

Mr Dennis Canavan, *Falkirk West*
Mr Mike Gapes, *Ilford South*
Mr David Harris, *St Ives*
Rt Hon Michael Jopling, *Westmorland and Lonsdale*
Mr Jim Lester, *Broxtowe*

Mr Ted Rowlands, *Merthyr Tydfil and Rhymney*
Rt Hon Peter Shore, *Bethnal Green and Stepney*
Rt Hon Sir John Stanley, *Tonbridge and Malling*
Mr David Sumberg, *Bury South*
Mr Robert Wareing, *Liverpool West Derby*

The cost of printing and publishing this Report is estimated by HMSO at £14,775.
The cost of preparing for publication the Shorthand Minutes taken before the Committee and published with this Report was £7,178.46.

TABLE OF CONTENTS

THIRD REPORT

THE EXPANDING RÔLE OF THE UNITED NATIONS AND ITS IMPLICATIONS FOR UNITED KINGDOM POLICY

The Foreign Affairs Committee has agreed to the following Report:

I. INTRODUCTION

1. From its headquarters in New York and Geneva the United Nations and its associated specialised agencies and organisations are directing efforts to rescue populations at risk of death, disease or starvation as a consequence of armed conflict, repression, internal strife or natural disaster in four of the world's six continents. In the last five years the United Nations has launched more peace-keeping operations than in the whole of the previous forty-three years of its history. The Foreign Secretary told the House on 12 May 1993 that "at the beginning of 1992 there were 10,000 United Nations peace-keeping troops; at the beginning of 1993 there were 60,000; and when the planned deployment in Mozambique happens there will be 100,000 in 12 separate operations".[1] Operations are taking place in India/Pakistan, Lebanon, Israel/Syria and Jerusalem, Cyprus, Cambodia, former Yugoslavia, Iraq/Kuwait, El Salvador, Western Sahara, Angola, Somalia and Mozambique. In addition there are at least another thirteen conflicts around the world where the UN is not currently deploying peace-keeping forces[2] although there are UN observer missions to some of them. Fifteen new peace-keeping operations have begun since 1987.[3] Peace-keeping operations are estimated to cost close to $3 billion in 1992, more than four times the previous highest annual figure.[4] The UK currently pays over 6 per cent of the cost of all peace-keeping operations through the system of assessed contributions. In the first three months of 1993 the UK has paid $57,804,461 to UN peace-keeping operations.[5] This compares with $90,549,248 in the whole of 1992.[6] Britain has contributed military personnel to five of the new operations (in former Yugoslavia, Namibia, Western Sahara, Iraq/Kuwait and Cambodia) and continues to provide forces to the operation in Cyprus. The net cost of UK military participation in these operations is estimated to be over £190 million for the five years since 1988[7] in addition to the UK's assessed contributions to peace-keeping and to the UN regular budget. In 1991–92 the UK contribution to the UN regular budget was £26,549,477 million and the UK contributed in total over £250 million to the UN and its associated agencies.[8]

2. On 31 January 1992 the first meeting of the UN Security Council at Head of State/Government level took place at the instigation of the Security Council Presidency, then held by the United Kingdom. The meeting symbolised the importance that the Organisation's Member States attached to the rôle of the United Nations in maintaining international peace and security in a world which, with the passing of the Cold War era, was entering, in the Prime Minister's words, "a time of great hope in international affairs, but also of uncertainty and potential instability".[9] This hope that the international community could do more to solve the world's problems, and the fears caused by growing instability and conflict in many parts of the world, especially within rather than between states, have combined to increase the demands on the United Nations. The Organisation is experiencing a major problem of under-capacity to achieve the tasks it has been set, and a related major problem of overcredibility: the more hopes that are placed in the UN, the greater the gap will become between expectations of the UN and what it can actually achieve.

3. At the same time, Dr Boutros Boutros-Ghali, who succeeded Mr Javier Perez de Cuellar as Secretary-General in January 1992, has seen it as his mission to reform the working of the Organisation and to increase its effectiveness. At the request of the Summit, he produced a report, *An Agenda for Peace*, published on 17 June 1992, on ways in which the UN could more

---

[1] HC Deb 12 May 1993, col 797.
[2] HC Deb 6 May 1993, col 180.
[3] See Annex D.
[4] Annual Report of the UN Secretary-General, September 1992.
[5] Official Report 17 May 1993, col 42W.
[6] HL Deb, 24 May 1993 WA col 2.
[7] HL Deb, 13 May 1993, WA cols 69-70.
[8] Ev.pp 63 and 65.
[9] Official Report, 3 February 1993 col 22.

effectively carry out its peace-keeping and peacemaking rôles. In the light of these events, the Committee decided to carry out an inquiry into the expanding tasks being performed by the United Nations and their implications for the United Kingdom and to make a contribution to the *Agenda for Peace* debate.[1]

SCOPE OF THE INQUIRY

4. The activities of the United Nations and its related organisations cover the whole world and a wide range of human activities. As the Foreign and Commonwealth Office pointed out at the start of our inquiry, its expanding rôle includes not only "threats to international peace and security, but such major issues as the environment, the protection and promotion of human rights, the effects of famine and mass migration and not least the problems of development".[2] It would have been impractical for us to have attempted to review the entire range of the organisation's work; we have for instance not dealt with the UN's important role in promoting arms control. Nor have we examined the work of the many specialised agencies of the UN in any detail except where it is directly relevant to our concerns; for instance, we have not considered the work of bodies such as the ILO (International Labour Organisation) or the Sustainable Development Commission established by the UN Conference on the Environment and Development last year.[3] Instead we decided to focus on those aspects highlighted by *An Agenda for Peace*, essentially the rôle of the Organisation in maintaining international peace and security. However, as the Security Council Summit made clear in its concluding statement, non-military sources of instability, in the humanitarian field among others, have become a threat to peace and security[4] and therefore we have addressed these issues as well.

5. It is clear that the UN's response to such threats encompasses not just the work of the Security Council (primarily responsible for international peace and security) but that of other UN organs, notably the work of the Secretariat (in preventive diplomacy and coordination of UN operations, for instance) and the humanitarian agencies (such as the UN High Commissioner for Refugees (UNHCR) and the UN Children's Fund (UNICEF). Organisations and arrangements outside the UN system, including non-governmental organisations (NGOs) and regional arrangements such as the European Community and NATO also have a part to play. Where appropriate, we comment on the rôles of such organisations in the work of the United Nations.

VISITS AND EVIDENCE

6. In the course of our inquiry we visited the United Nations headquarters in New York and Geneva and three regions where there are currently large United Nations operations: former Yugoslavia, Cambodia and Somalia. A brief summary of the visits to former Yugoslavia, Cambodia and Somalia can be found in Annex A. We took formal evidence from Mr Douglas Hurd, Secretary of State for Foreign and Commonwealth Affairs, Baroness Chalker, Minister for Overseas Development, Mr Douglas Hogg, Minister of State, Foreign and Commonwealth Office and FCO officials, Ministry of Defence officials, Lord Owen, Co-Chairman of the International Conference on the former Yugoslavia, Mr Mohammed Sahnoun, formerly the Secretary-General's Special Representative in Somalia, representatives of NGOs and a number of academic experts and commentators. We held a number of informal meetings at Westminster with distinguished visitors; these are listed at Annex B. We also received a large amount of written evidence, much of which is published in the appendices to the Minutes of Evidence.

7. We have been assisted in our inquiry by Mr David Travers of the Department of Politics and International Relations at Lancaster University. We are extremely grateful for his help.

II THE KEY ISSUES

8. After many years in which the UN was not always regarded as the principal forum for settling international disputes, it is currently experiencing the opposite problem of being expected

---

[1] The Select Committee on Defence has also inquired into United Kingdom Peace-keeping and Intervention Forces this session. Third Report from the Select Committee on Defence, United Kingdom Peacekeeping and Intervention Forces, HC 389, 1992–93.
[2] Ev.p 4.
[3] The Committee has taken evidence in a separate inquiry from the Director General of the UN Educational, Scientific and Cultural Organisation (UNESCO) (HC 690–i; 1992–93).
[4] quoted in Ev.p 299.

to cope with all the world's crises. In the Secretary-General's words, "Nations and peoples increasingly are looking to the United Nations for assistance in keeping the peace—and holding it responsible when this cannot be so".[1]

9. A growing number of the crises in which the UN's services are called upon occur *within* states rather than between them, or occur in countries where the most basic framework of the state has disappeared. One superpower, the USSR, has broken up into fifteen republics, between (and within) which tensions are growing and in some cases conflict is taking place. One European state, Yugoslavia, has been replaced by a number of states plunged into bloody wars which have proved difficult to classify as internal or international. Somalia collapsed from dictatorship to almost complete anarchy, and other countries in Africa are at risk. There is ongoing concern about gross violations of human rights by governments in many parts of the world towards their populations as, for example, in Iraq where the UN has intervened to protect humanitarian relief and to provide a degree of security for threatened populations.

10. There is nothing new about wars, civil wars and ruthless dictatorships, and indeed the UN has in the past become involved in internal conflicts, as in the Congo crisis in 1960. However, there has recently been a fundamental shift in assumptions about the extent to which the UN should become involved in such situations, following years of much greater hesitation when all proposals for intervention were judged on their Cold War implications. Although the UN Charter is founded on respect for the sovereignty of states, and the techniques laid down in the Charter for dealing with international conflict are based firmly on the idea of the state; with the Cold War constraints removed there are more and more demands for the UN to override national sovereignty where there is a perceived need to relieve suffering and bring about peace and security. Thus worldwide expectations have been raised about the UN's capacity to confront these situations and the Organisation has found itself addressing the problems of how to deal with conflicts not only between states, but within them, and indeed within fragments of former states as well. All this has demanded new thinking about the doctrine of humanitarian intervention, which is still far from universally agreed.

11. Not only is there a greater expectation that the "international community" should "do something", there is a greater awareness of the horrors of the modern world due to the expansion and increasing sophistication of the electronic media. Television allows dramatic pictures of human misery to be shown all over the world almost while events are taking place, which has led to a change in the public's perception of the world: the growth of television means that there are fewer far away countries of which we know little. Of course, television is selective and it is usually the case that, if Bosnia is dominating the screen, Somalia or the Sudan will not be noticed. Even within countries, public perception of events may be coloured by where the television cameras happen, or are allowed, to be. Nevertheless, television coverage has a huge effect on the pressure members of the public put on parliamentarians and governments, which in turn may affect the policy of governments.

12. **These increased expectations of what the UN can and should do raise fundamental questions:**

> **Will the UN emerge as the major global power acting in its own right or as legitimiser of actions by alliances of Member States? How far can expansion of the UN's authority coexist with states' traditional independent pursuit of their own foreign policy objectives?**

> **What criteria should the UN use to decide when it should become involved in internal conflict; and on what grounds should it intervene in sovereign states without consent, especially when that intervention involves the use of force? How far will the UN be able to implement internationally agreed solutions which are negotiated by or with the UN? Can the UN be seen to be acting in a consistent and even-handed manner?**

> **If the UN is given a larger role, is it equipped to deliver the service that Member States expect of it? Is the organisation's bureaucracy sufficiently flexible and able to adapt to meet the demands placed on it? Can it rely on the necessary financial, military and civilian support from Member States, and will they provide the necessary political will? How should the UN handle the increasing number of peace-keeping operations which are faltering and where there are calls for them to be further reinforced?**

---

[1] *An Agenda for Peace*, para 47.

III AN AGENDA FOR PEACE

13. In response to the new challenges facing the UN, the Security Council Summit commissioned the Secretary-General to produce a report on ways of "strengthening and making more efficient the capacity of the United Nations for preventive diplomacy, for peacemaking and for peace-keeping".[1] In his report, *An Agenda for Peace*, the Secretary-General considered these points and added some of his own, including "post-conflict peace-building". He sees the UN as working in a changing international context, in which the UN has a new rôle to play in ensuring the security of the world.[2] His report was welcomed by the Security Council, and the Foreign Secretary called it "an important collection of proposals" which should be followed up swiftly.[3]

14. It is not our intention to comment in detail on all his analyses and recommendations (which are summarised in Annex C) nor to confine ourselves solely to the issues he addresses. In this Report we examine the range of UN engagement in international crises, commenting on his proposals and relating them where appropriate to other areas of the UN's work which are not addressed in *An Agenda for Peace*. One area which he regards as crucial to the success of the UN's peace endeavours is the proper financing of UN peace-keeping operations. The present crisis in the funding of the UN goes much wider than the peace-keeping budget, as the Secretary-General recognises.[4] Given the overwhelming importance of that subject it is treated in a separate section (paras 158–176 below).

15. The United Nations Charter distinguishes clearly between "the pacific settlement of disputes", means for which are set out in Chapter VI of the Charter, and "action with respect to threats to the peace, breaches of the peace, and acts of aggression", which includes the use of military force, set out in Chapter VII of the Charter. The terms used in *An Agenda for Peace* by the Secretary-General and the definitions he employs to describe the UN's methods of operation overlap and do not always match the situation on the ground. In *An Agenda for Peace* he defines three "integrally related" terms:

> "*Preventive diplomacy* is action to prevent disputes from arising between parties, to prevent existing disputes from escalating into conflicts and to limit the spread of the latter when they occur.
>
> *Peacemaking* is action to bring hostile parties to agreement, essentially through such peaceful means as those foreseen in Chapter VI of the United Nations Charter.
>
> *Peace-keeping* is the deployment of a United Nations presence in the field, hitherto with the consent of all the parties concerned, normally involving United Nations military and/or police personnel and frequently civilians as well. Peace-keeping is a technique that expands the possibilities for both the prevention of conflict and the making of peace."[5]

He also describes:

> "the critically related concept of post-conflict *peace-building*—action to identify and support structures which will tend to strengthen and solidify peace in order to avoid a relapse into conflict. Preventive diplomacy seeks to resolve disputes before violence breaks out; peacemaking and peace-keeping are required to halt conflicts and preserve peace once it is attained. If successful, they strengthen the opportunity for post-conflict peace-building, which can prevent the recurrence of violence among nations and peoples."[6]

16. All four definitions have attracted comment. *Preventive diplomacy* has normally been used in the sense of the United Nations providing conciliatory help on a neutral basis. But the Secretary-General has extended the concept to include the use of military forces in a (possibly one-sided) deterrent rôle.

---

[1] *An Agenda for Peace*, para 1.
[2] *Ibid*, paras 8–16.
[3] Ev.p 2.
[4] *An Agenda for Peace*, paras 69–74.
[5] *An Agenda for Peace*, para 20.
[6] *An Agenda for Peace*, para 21.

17. While the Secretary-General's definition of *peacemaking* in *An Agenda for Peace* refers to action *"essentially* through. peaceful means", in the section on peacemaking in the body of his report he discusses not only peaceful actions by the General Assembly, the Security Council, the Secretary-General and the International Court of Justice, but also enforcement measures under Chapter VII—economic sanctions and the use of military force (including an innovation, peace enforcement units). So peacemaking in his terms blurs the distinction between Chapter VI—consent—and Chapter VII—enforcement—as well as involving both military and non-military action. Therefore the fundamental distinction between peaceful means of settlement in Chapter VI of the Charter and the enforcement provisions of Chapter VII has been lost. The fact that "peacemaking" is often confused with "peace enforcement" is perhaps understandable given the ambiguity in the Secretary-General's report. In this Report we have used the phrase "peace enforcement" rather than "peacemaking" to avoid any ambiguity.

18. The Secretary-General's definition of *peace-keeping* includes the phrase *"hitherto* with the consent of the parties concerned". This has raised fears that the nature of peace-keeping as a non-violent, non-threatening activity might be changing because consent had always been regarded as an essential prerequisite. The United Nations Association[1] believed that this raised important issues about the criteria for such intervention, and the safety of peacekeepers deployed on operations where consent had not been given.

19. The chapter in *An Agenda for Peace* on *post-conflict peacebuilding* differs markedly from the earlier chapters. Its main focus is on those peace-keeping operations which have helped to bring about the ending of civil strife. Although the Secretary-General makes no specific recommendations, he makes the claim that there is a new requirement for technical assistance in rebuilding societies which the United Nations has an obligation to develop and provide when requested. This includes support for the transformation of deficient national structures and capabilities, and for the strengthening of new democratic institutions.

20. One witness was concerned at the Secretary-General's definition of peacebuilding as a post-conflict activity. Brigadier Michael Harbottle, Director of the Centre for International Peacebuilding, argued that peacebuilding is the third dimension, along with peacemaking and peace-keeping, of the peaceful settlement of disputes:

> "It is required in the preventive diplomacy of the pre-conflict phase; it is performed by UN peacekeepers as an important part of their rôle in working to restore, maintain and ensure the civil human rights of the people in the conflict area ... and their right to normal existence ... Peacebuilding is all embracing and should not be limited."[2]

21. Clearly the definitions used in *An Agenda for Peace* have not gained widespread acceptance. If anything, they have caused confusion. The Secretary of State for Defence (Mr Rifkind) has voiced a common attitude: there were "real difficulties" in finding satisfactory and mutually exclusive definitions for peacemaking, peace-keeping and peace enforcement. He suggested a general definition for all these activities: "the collective use of military action by the international community to help resolve security disputes both within and between states".[3] The Foreign Secretary (Mr Hurd) has said that peace-keeping is "the new label on something which goes back at least as far as the activities of the Roman army at the height of the Roman empire".[4] However, it is important to try and maintain some distinction between the various UN activities in the field of international peace and security, not least because the level of support given by Member States may depend on the exact nature of the action involved.

22. In this Report we employ the Secretary-General's terms where they are helpful but have not been tied down by them. There are other ways of approaching the problem of definitions. The various methods of preventing or resolving conflict discussed by the Secretary-General can also be grouped in three basic categories, defined by the techniques to be used, rather than by their purpose. First, there are techniques of UN involvement which are diplomatic and civilian and do not involve the military, such as preventive diplomacy. The second category consists of techniques using the military, but where soldiers are armed primarily for self-defensive purposes: preventive deployment, protection of humanitarian relief operations and traditional

---

[1] Ev. p 268.
[2] Ev. p 255.
[3] 'Peacekeeping or peacemaking', RUSI Journal April 1993 p. 1.
[4] 'Foreign Policy and International Security' RUSI Journal, December 1992 p 3.

peace-keeping fall within this category. The third category is the use of the military in an active rôle. Such enforcement actions include the coalition action in the Gulf and the US-led, now UN-run operation in Somalia.

23. Although the Secretary-General, in *An Agenda for Peace*, and the UN Charter set out a fairly clear range of escalating options for the UN in dealing with conflicts, on the ground the categories have become blurred, as for example in Bosnia. The Secretary-General recognises this to some extent, stating that diplomacy will continue throughout the spectrum of activities from fact-finding through to military action, while a UN deployment can serve to prevent conflict and start the work of peace-building.[1] These are all different techniques for carrying out the UN's wishes. They are not part of a rigid sequence of events; the way in which the spectrum of UN activity actually unfolds on the ground is multi-stranded, complex and often confused.

24. The sequence of events can take a number of different courses. First, and continuing throughout any dispute, there is factfinding by the Secretary-General, and early warning of potential dangers. If a problem is detected, the Secretary-General may try to resolve it by private diplomacy. If he considers this will not work, he refers it to the Security Council (or it is referred by a Member State). The Council can call on the parties to agree to mediation, or, with the consent of the parties, it can station monitors or even a preventive military force. Whatever means are used to prevent conflict, once a stable situation is achieved the UN may become involved in peacebuilding measures designed to ensure, on a long-term basis, that the danger of conflict does not arise again. Second, if the diplomacy is unsuccessful, and conflict occurs, the UN may decide to provide humanitarian aid and use diplomacy to stop the fighting. If the fighting stops, peacekeepers may be deployed and the peacebuilding process is carried out as above. Thirdly, the UN may decide to use force to stop the fighting or reverse the conquest or oppression being carried out. At that point Chapter VII enforcement may be used, either by the UN or by states acting on its behalf. If that action drives the parties to agreement, or stops the aggressor, the process can then continue as before. Throughout all this the process of diplomacy will carry on and there may be a continuing humanitarian effort. There is thus a number of different routes any UN engagement can take, each involving different UN activities, or a different combination of activities.

IV EXPERIENCES AND PROBLEMS

1945–1987

25. The United Nations was established in 1945 with the principal aim of maintaining international peace and security. Primary responsibility was given to the Security Council, although the General Assembly and the Secretary-General were also given important rôles. The Security Council takes decisions on behalf of all the members of the United Nations. The Council has the legal authority to take decisions that are binding on all Member States of the United Nations and to a limited extent non-members. The Council must be able to function at any time.[2]

26. Chapter VI of the Charter sets out the means by which the Council may by recommendation assist in settling disputes that threaten to endanger the peace. Chapter VII contains provisions by which the Council may deal with threats to, or breaches of, the peace. It may either make recommendations or issue orders. It may take provisional measures, such as calling for a ceasefire; if this is ignored it may use economic and diplomatic sanctions and if these prove inadequate the Council may threaten to use or actually use military forces placed at its disposal by Member States.

27. Until 1987, however, the Council seldom played the central rôle envisaged for it in the Charter; this rôle was to a limited extent fulfilled by the Secretary-General and the General Assembly. First, due to the onset of the Cold War, the permanent members were unable to agree on what armed forces the United Nations should possess and thus the special agreements which had been envisaged between the Member States and the Security Council about supplying these forces were never negotiated. Thus a central deterrent against aggression was stillborn. Secondly the Council was rarely in a position to declare that international peace and

---

[1] *An Agenda for Peace*, para 45.
[2] See paras 180 and 181 for a fuller description of the Security Council.

security had been threatened or breached, despite the widespread international violence, and civil violence with international implications, that had taken place, because of the use of the veto by the permanent members. And thirdly even when there was transient agreement the Council was wary of taking decisions under Chapter VII because it was concerned as to whether Member States would enforce them.

28. The outcome was that between 1945 and 1990 the Security Council explicitly declared that international peace was threatened or breached in only five situations: Palestine in 1948; Korea in 1950 (in the temporary absence from the Council of the Soviet Union); Southern Rhodesia in 1966 and 1978; South Africa in 1977 and the Falklands in 1982. Mandatory sanctions were used twice against Southern Rhodesia between 1966 and 1977 and an arms embargo against South Africa since 1977. The use of force was only authorised on three occasions: in Korea, when the Council recommended that United Nations members furnish such assistance to the Republic of Korea as might be necessary to repel the armed attack and to restore international peace and security to the area; in the Congo in 1961 when the Council permitted the peace-keeping force to use force if necessary to prevent civil war and to apprehend "military and paramilitary personnel in the Congo not under United Nations command, and mercenaries"; and against Southern Rhodesia in 1966, when the Council called upon the United Kingdom to prevent, by the use of force if necessary, the arrival at Beira of vessels reasonably believed to be carrying oil destined for Southern Rhodesia.

29. When violence was threatened or used and when the Security Council was able to act it tended to base its decisions on Chapter VI rather than Chapter VII of the Charter. It urged and persuaded rather than ordered and enforced. On occasions it authorised the use of military personnel provided by governments of Member States, directed by the Secretary-General and partially paid for by the United Nations when the money was available. These forces were used to observe ceasefires, to separate combatants, and to help maintain internal law and order where its breakdown might have threatened international peace and security. But these observers, who were unarmed, and the peacekeepers who normally could only use force in self defence, could only be deployed *with the permission of the host state*. In many instances, while the soldiers helped to maintain calm, the politicians were unable to solve the underlying dispute despite valiant attempts to help by the Secretary-General or his representatives and concerned states. Thus some peace-keeping operations, such as those in the Middle East, the Indian sub-continent and Cyprus, have almost become permanent features of the international landscape, helping to maintain a peace, while the UN remains unable to promote a long term settlement because of the intractability of the political problem which gave rise to the violence.

UN OPERATIONS SINCE 1987

30. In 1987, however, the permanent members began to develop a collegiate attitude, partly because of the improved relations between the United States and the Soviet Union and their more favourable attitude to the efficacy of the Security Council, possibly partly because of a British suggestion that the permanent members should meet regularly for informal discussions and partly because the then Secretary-General, Mr Javier Perez de Cuellar, helped to persuade the Council to alter its working practices and to adopt a common policy towards obtaining an effective ceasefire in the Iran-Iraq war.

31. Since then, the Security Council has played a significant rôle in dealing with international disputes in which it has expanded the meaning of threats to international peace and security to include international terrorism and humanitarian concerns. It has now begun to use the wide range of methods available to it under the Charter. It has tried to prevent disputes emerging by encouraging the Secretary-General to engage in preventive diplomacy, or by undertaking fact-finding missions itself, some of which have been concerned with ethnic problems within a state. It has supported the Secretary-General's work with regional organisations, interested parties and the permanent members to bring about negotiated settlements to many disputes, particularly internal ones, that have threatened international peace in areas such as Central America, the Balkans and Cambodia. **The Security Council has created 15 peace-keeping operations since 1988, many of them large, complex and expensive, to support or verify negotiated settlements.** These have involved police and civilians in addition to military personnel performing traditional peace-keeping rôles.

32. *Unarmed observers* have been employed in:

Afghanistan (UNGOMAP) to verify the withdrawal of Soviet armed forces after the signing of the Geneva Accords in April 1988;

Iran-Iraq (UNIIMOG) to monitor the ceasefire line and the return of the armed force of each state to the internationally recognised boundaries;

Angola (UNAVEM I) to oversee the withdrawal of Cuban troops according to a timetable agreed between the parties which was an agreed precondition to the holding of elections in Namibia;

Former Yugoslavia (UNPROFOR) to monitor the air exclusion zone and report any violations of it;[1]

Central America (ONUCA) to verify that aid to irregular forces had ceased and that the territory of one state was not being used for attacks upon other states; and

Somalia (UNOSOM I) where UN observers attempted to monitor the ceasefire between the armed factions within the country.

33. *Armed UN soldiers* have been deployed in Croatia (UNPROFOR), where troops are monitoring the ceasefire and the demilitarized protected areas (UNPAs) following the withdrawal of the Yugoslav National Army (JNA), and Kuwait/Iraq (UNIKOM). In these operations a combination of armed and unarmed military personnel have been deployed. Originally the operation in Kuwait/Iraq was an unarmed observer mission, protected by armed infantry, deployed under Chapter VII at the end of the enforcement operations which had secured the liberation of Kuwait from the Iraqi invasion. Although it did not under its mandate require the consent of all the parties, in practice it could not work without their cooperation. Its purposes were to monitor the Khor Abdullah waterway and the demilitarised zone between Iraq and Kuwait and to observe any hostile or potentially hostile action mounted from the territory of either state. The observers reported Iraqi violations to the Security Council, which took counter measures, authorising the strengthening of the force by armed infantry and permitting it to prevent physically, and if necessary redress, violations of the border or demilitarised zone.[2] This is an operation which had its basis in a Chapter VII action to redress the violation of a member state's sovereignty, and is an unusual blend of "traditional" peace-keeping and enforcement.

34. A third type of operation undertaken in recent years is multi-functional, bringing together military, police and civilian personnel to help in the implementation of an agreement which has been reached between parties (sometimes with the assistance of the UN acting as mediator). Frequently these have been internal disputes with international implications—UN involvement in such activities has grown considerably since the end of the Cold War.

35. The first such operation was in Namibia (UNTAG). Currently there are similar operations in Angola, Cambodia, El Salvador, Mozambique and Western Sahara.[3] The various activities carried out during these operations can be grouped under functional headings:

Military: monitoring ceasefires, cantonment and demobilisation of troops, location and destruction of weapons, demining, reform and retraining of armed forces, protecting borders, investigating claims of the presence of foreign forces, providing security for elections and helping rebuild infrastructure.

Police: visiting police stations, monitoring police activities, investigating alleged humans rights violations by national police forces, training new police forces, enforcing arrests of suspected criminals and protecting the electoral process.

Human rights: monitoring human rights, conducting human rights education programmes and investigating human rights violations.

Information: explaining the peace settlement, the reasons for the UN deployment and the opportunities for the future of the country.

[1] Members of the Committee met a team of UN military observers monitoring the air exclusion zone in Pristina during their visit to Kosovo; see para 53 below
[2] Official Report, 17 May 1993 col 47W
[3] A list of UN peacekeeping and observation missions is at Annex D.

Elections: the UN's involvement can range from simple observation and verification, through supervision and control of nationally conducted elections up to the organisation and conduct of elections by the UN itself.

Rehabilitation: the UN has helped in many cases to rehabilitate and reconstruct a state, both in the short term and through longer-term development projects.

Repatriation: the UN has arranged for the return and resettlement of hundreds of thousands of refugees.

Administration: supervising or controlling the administration within states. The UN Transitional Authority in Cambodia (UNTAC), for instance, was mandated to control foreign affairs, national defence, public security, finance and information in an attempt to create, sustain and monitor a neutral political environment for elections to take place.[1]

36. The fourth type of peace-keeping is innovatory: the use of military personnel to protect the delivery of humanitarian aid. This was attempted in Somalia (UNOSOM I) in 1992; the operation was a failure and was replaced first by the Unified Task Force (UNITAF) then by UNOSOM II, both of which worked under a Chapter VII mandate which authorised force to be used, if necessary, to achieve the objectives of the operation. A major humanitarian protection operation has been carried out by UNPROFOR in Bosnia.

37. The Council has also used the provisions of Chapter VII of the Charter more than ever before. It demanded a ceasefire and withdrawal of forces in the Iran-Iraq war. It has used sanctions against Iraq, Yugoslavia, Somalia, Libya, Liberia, Rwanda, the Khmer Rouge and may do so against Haiti. It authorised Member States to use force against Iraq to enforce Security Council resolutions, and subsequently demanded the destruction of certain types of weapons and established a long-term monitoring programme there. The UN has also established a compensation commission which is intended to settle claims against the Iraqi government[2] and is controlling Baghdad's international trade. The UN boundary commission has demarcated the disputed border between the two states and this border is to be protected by the UN.

38. In Somalia, in the absence of a government, the Security Council has authorised the use of force to ensure that humanitarian assistance was safely delivered to the needy and, with the handover from the United States to the UN in May 1993, for the first time the Secretary-General is directing a force which from the outset has had a Chapter VII mandate. The UNOSOM II operation in Somalia is similar to other peacebuilding operations, but with the crucial difference that the troops concerned are allowed to use force if necessary to achieve the UN's objectives. Its mandate includes ceasefire monitoring, demobilisation and disarming of forces, assisting in settlement of political disputes and encouraging national reconciliation leading towards elections, creating new and durable political and administrative institutions (including a new police force), repatriation and resettlement of refugees and economic assistance.

39. From such activities the idea of a new kind of operation is emerging: not peace-keeping in the accepted sense but nearer to peace enforcement, or enforcement of agreed boundaries possibly within a federal state. It is a more forcible variant of "traditional" peace-keeping. Parties have to agree to a plan and the composition, commander and mandate of the force to be used, but the military in such operations will have the power to use force in circumstances other than self-defence. Where political leaders have entered into an agreement in good faith, but do not have complete control over the military and other factions in a conflict, if the agreement is to be maintained, the UN may have to authorise the use of force to prevent any potential violations or redress any breaches of the agreed plan.[3]

40. Alongside all this activity there are some important concerns. The Security Council can only work if the permanent members allow it to do so. There is an emerging debate about the composition and size of the Security Council in which it may be very difficult to reconcile representation with effectiveness. There is a view that the Security Council has taken action, particularly decisions to authorise the use of force under Chapter VII, on a selective basis, influenced by the interests of Member States, rather than adopting an evenhanded approach.

---

[1] For text of the Paris Agreement see Cm 1786 (1991).
[2] SCR 687 (1991).
[3] Marrack Goulding: The evolution of United Nations Peacekeeping, Cyril Foster lecture 1993, Oxford, 4 March 1993.

There is unease among some members about the degree to which the changing meaning of international peace and security has allowed the Security Council to intervene in internal affairs and reduce the freedom of action of governments. There is concern that non-members of the Security Council do not have enough influence on its decisions. There is also concern that military enforcement operations by the UN may depend excessively on the United States' willingness to take part, because of the sheer weight and dominance of US financial and military power. This puts an enormous burden and responsibility on the USA itself. Doubts have been expressed as to whether the Secretariat is adequately staffed and equipped to undertake the more extensive rôle that Member States appear to be demanding of it. There is a fear that the United Nations is now overstretched, particularly in the peace-keeping field, where the Council is in almost daily session dealing with the problems posed by uncooperative parties whose support is essential to the success of the operations, where the Secretariat is trying to manage many different operations at the same time and where members are facing difficulties in providing the necessary manpower and paying the greatly increased contributions. The next section of this Report examines in more detail the way in which the UN has responded, or might respond to these challenges, drawing on our discussions during our visits as well as on the formal evidence we have received.

V HOW THE UN RESPONDS TO CHALLENGES

PREVENTIVE DIPLOMACY

41. The Secretary-General lays great stress in *An Agenda for Peace* on preventive diplomacy as a means for tackling crises at the earliest stage. The British government also recognise its significance—the Foreign Secretary has said that "primary healthcare costs less than hospital treatment", a view shared by many of those we met in our meetings at the United Nations in New York.[1] The Secretary-General states in *An Agenda for Peace* that preventive diplomacy requires measures to create confidence; it needs early warning based on information gathering and informal and formal fact-finding; and it might also involve preventive deployment and, in some situations, demilitarised zones.[2] He also proposes that **regional organisations** could play a greater part in developing confidence-building measures and offers to undertake periodic consultations with parties to disputes and with regional organisations.[3] However, he recognises that there are difficulties in putting such ideas into practice. First, states must have the political will to undertake confidence building measures, yet those with deep-seated mutual antipathies may be the least likely to undertake them. Secondly, appropriate regional organisations are not present in all parts of the globe (for example in the Far East); their membership does not always contain the most important states in the region; some political problems affecting them are caused by extra-regional states; and some lack the political and administrative capacity to encourage confidence-building measures. Thirdly, it is not clear how deep a reservoir of confidence-building knowledge the Secretariat can draw upon.

42. The Secretary-General proposes an extension of the UN's **fact-finding** capacity to provide the UN with timely and accurate factual knowledge on social and economic trends as well as political developments.[4] The British Government supports this proposal, stressing the importance of Article 99 of the Charter, under which the Secretary-General may "bring to the attention of the Council any matter which in his opinion may threaten the maintenance of international peace and security". The Foreign Secretary has suggested that "we must build up Article 99".[5] The Secretary-General has used Article 99 in three different ways.[6] First, if the Secretary-General is to be able to consider whether any matter might threaten international peace and security, and if he is to provide early warning, he must be able to make an informed independent judgement. He therefore consults ceaselessly, conducts research, seeks opinions from the Organisation's legal staff, tours capital cities, responds to requests for visits from troubled government leaders, appoints special representatives and stations staff in areas of tension with the permission of the host government, and sends expert fact-finding teams to discover, for example, whether prohibited weapons have been used (for example the mission to Nagorno-Karabakh in July 1992 investigated but failed to substantiate Azerbaijani claims that Armenia had used chemical weapons).

---

[1] Official Report, 23 February 1993 col 785.
[2] *An Agenda for Peace*, para 23.
[3] *Ibid* para 24.
[4] *Ibid* para 25.
[5] 'Foreign Policy and International Security', *RUSI Journal* 1992, p 3.
[6] See Ev.pp 336ff.

43. Secondly, Article 99 has also contributed in part to the shaping of **"good offices"** diplomacy by the Secretary-General to respond to any unexpected demands upon his office and to unexpected events. It has usually initially been undertaken by the Secretary-General without a formal mandate from the political organs. Demands for this service have come from Member States and non-state entities and individuals; on occasions the Secretary-General has offered his services either privately or publicly. Examples of Dr Boutros-Ghali's independent diplomacy include sending an envoy to Indonesia in February 1992 to obtain information about events in East Timor on 12 November 1991 and sending a fact-finding mission to Moldova in June 1992.[1] The political organs, the Economic and Social Council and the Human Rights Commission have, additionally, delegated good offices and other diplomatic and fact-finding tasks to the Secretary-General and his special representatives or envoys. Sometimes when a Security Council resolution has aroused controversy, the Secretary-General has detached himself from the delegation and executed the mandate on his own authority, and on occasions the Secretary-General has stimulated a good offices mission from the Security Council (a recent example being Dr Boutros-Ghali's response to the violent events in South Africa in June 1992). **We agree with the Secretary-General that a UN fact-finding mission can help to defuse a dispute by its presence, indicating to the parties that the organisation, and in particular the Security Council, is actively seized of the matter as a present or potential threat to international security.**

44. The third way in which the Secretary-General has used Article 99 is its formal use: to call the **Security Council** into urgent session on his own responsibility. The Secretary-General for practical, legal and political reasons has formally invoked Article 99 on only three occasions: the Congo in 1960 (Hammarskjöld); the United States' diplomatic hostages in Iran in 1979 (Waldheim) and the increased violence in Lebanon in 1989 (Perez de Cuellar). But he has used Article 99 in an implied form in a variety of ways, when faced with potential or actual threats to the peace, to stimulate action from the Council or to express his concern.[2]

45. Past and present Secretaries General have argued that the Secretary-General should be given greater powers to improve his effectiveness in the field of preventive diplomacy. Mr Perez de Cuellar believed that the General Assembly should grant the Secretary-General the authority under Article 96 to seek an advisory opinion from the International Court of Justice. If the parties failed to refer the matter to the Court, an advisory opinion sought by the Secretary-General might contribute to a fair settlement. Such authority would strengthen the rôle of the Secretary-General in preventive diplomacy.[3] Dr Boutros-Ghali would like the Secretary-General and expert human rights bodies to be empowered to bring massive violations of human rights to the attention of the Security Council with recommendations for action.[4]

46. We also received evidence about ways of improving the quality and the scope of **information available to the Secretary-General**. One way might be for the Secretary-General to have a rudimentary diplomatic service. In the past, representatives of the Secretary-General have reported temporarily from trouble spots—Mr Dag Hammarskjöld, for instance, made appointments to Laos and Jordan. Mr Perez de Cuellar, however, established political offices in Kabul, Islamabad, Tehran and Baghdad. Dr Boutros-Ghali has created interim offices in some of the states of the former Soviet Union; if the number of such offices were expanded, the Secretary-General might be able to receive a flow of reliable information from his own staff stationed around the world. But it is possible that members might object to the increased cost involved. Dr Paul Taylor of the London School of Economics suggested that States should negotiate a network of treaties guaranteeing a right of access to their territories for United Nations inspectors during potential crises.[5]

47. Dr Boutros-Ghali, in *An Agenda for Peace*[6], argues that the Secretary-General should be able to take advantage of the **early warning mechanisms** of the Specialised Agencies and the United Nations functional offices: information which they obtained concerning environmental threats, the risk of nuclear accident, natural disasters, mass movements of populations, the threat of famine and the spread of disease needed to be placed in a political context to assess whether peace was threatened, and how the United Nations might alleviate any such threat. Sir

---

[1] See Ev.pp 345ff.
[2] Ev. pp 346–357.
[3] Annual Report for 1991 p 11.
[4] Annual Report for 1992 para 101 p 38.
[5] Ev. p 187.
[6] Para 26.

Crispin Tickell was doubtful whether the Secretary-General would obtain the close cooperation of the Specialised Agencies: "He has not got the power to intervene and he has not got the power to bang heads together, although many of us sometimes wish that the Secretary-General had such power".[1]

48. The Secretary-General might be assisted by closer **intelligence** links with the secretariats of regional organisations, or regular briefings by the intelligence agencies of the permanent members on questions affecting the maintenance of international peace and security. One witness argued that the Military Staff Committee might offer military intelligence and in particular supplementary information to that contained in the United Nations arms transfer register.[2] (Ministry of Defence witnesses noted that the term "intelligence" was not generally used in the UN, as it had the wrong connotations for the organisation. It was generally referred to as "collection of military information".[3]) Dr Taylor suggested that the Secretary-General might have independent access to information from **satellites**—a "Global Watch"—if members were willing to bear the expense.[4] If this were to be arranged the Organisation would also have to hire the expertise to interpret the data. A precedent has already been established: UNSCOM leased a U2 plane from the United States to overfly Iraq regularly and the expertise to interpret the photographs.[5] FCO witnesses were, however, cautious about the extent to which the work of UNSCOM created a precedent for intrusive inspection, noting the wariness of Third World countries about the intrusive powers granted to the Commission.[6]

49. There is a convention that the Secretary-General has to request information from, rather than having it pressed on him by, governments if he is to remain impartial and independent. But a number of United Nations' bodies have already benefitted from national intelligence including that of the United Kingdom. The Chairman of the Special Commission on the disarming of Iraq (UNSCOM) has been provided with valuable information which he has filtered before passing it on to his officials. Indeed, Dr David Kay, formerly an inspection team member for UNSCOM, has pointed out the vital function performed by the Special Commission in legitimising the passage of national intelligence information to an international body.[7] Similarly, Hans Blix, the Director General of the International Atomic Energy Agency, has been informed about possible violations of the nuclear non-proliferation treaty and the international nuclear safeguards system. This information is held in a special cell within the Director General's office to prevent premature disclosure, a practice which the Secretary-General could follow. Member States have provided the sanctions monitoring committees with intelligence information about alleged violations.

50. **We agree that the Secretary-General should have access to the best possible information to enable him to do his job. We recommend that the UK Government discuss with the Secretary-General and the other permanent members of the Security Council the feasibility of providing him with information held by national intelligence agencies so that the UN is better aware of potential threats to international peace and security.**

51. It is also important for the UN Secretariat to be able to collect, collate and assess information relating to preventive diplomacy and early warning if it is to make good use of it. The FCO told us that there was no single Department in the United Nations specifically devoted to preventive diplomacy, though in practice the Department of Political Affairs took the lead. Within UN Headquarters in New York, the Department of Humanitarian Affairs and the Department of Peace-keeping Operations also have a rôle to play. There are 26 desk officers for geographical areas in the Department of Political Affairs working on aspects of preventive diplomacy. A system of duty officers provides 24 hour coverage. The Department of Peace-keeping Operations is now establishing a situation room manned around the clock.[8] Under-Secretary General Goulding is engaged in a review of the structure of the Department of Political Affairs which might lead to an increase in its staff if it proved possible to re-deploy people from elsewhere in the Secretariat. **We recommend that the UK Government exert pressure**

[1] Q 359.
[2] Q 407.
[3] Q 478.
[4] Ev.pp 187–88.
[5] *Bulletin of Arms Control*, August 1992 p 5.
[6] Ev.p 61.
[7] *Bulletin of Arms Control*, August 1992 p 6; see also Ev.p 309–310.
[8] Ev.pp 360.

for the UN Secretariat to be reorganised. We believe staff should be deployed from other, less vital, areas of the UN Secretariat, to increase the capacity of the Department of Political Affairs in preventive diplomacy.

52. If the potential of preventive diplomacy is fulfilled the Secretary-General and his senior colleagues might be able to maintain a watching global brief, remove friction, undertake good offices and help solve disputes on a greater scale than hitherto. He might also be able to have informal consultations with members of the Security Council on developments before they become threats and before members have to adopt positions.[1] Dr Taylor believed that for the first time real progress could be made towards creating doubts in the minds of potential malefactors that they were seen, that the attention of the world was on them, and that their intentions were understood. This, he thought, would represent a qualitative change in the rôle of mechanisms for the maintenance of international peace and security.[2] **Preventive diplomacy, even backed up by more effective mechanisms for the provision of information and analysis to the Secretary-General should not be seen as a panacea. Even were the Secretariat to be fully informed and the Secretary-General to draw the attention of the Security Council to potential crises, the essential elements in any timely and effective United Nations action are the political will to act upon that information, the capacity to execute the decision and favourable responses from the disputants. Preventive diplomacy must also be backed up by a determination by the Security Council to take tougher action if the parties fail to respond.**

PREVENTIVE DEPLOYMENT AND DEMILITARIZED ZONES

53. Witnesses generally welcomed the idea of the preventive deployment of UN troops where this would remove the likelihood of hostilities or deter conflict.[3] The concept of preventive deployment is not new, but its application in circumstances where conflict has not broken out is an innovation. Some of the instances of deployment of unarmed United Nations military observers (UNMOs) may also be regarded as preventive deployment: for example the deployment of UNMOs to monitor the no fly zone over Bosnia, some of whom are based at Pristina military airfield in Serbia. United Nations observers in Azerbaijan to monitor events in Nagorno Karabakh or in South Africa to monitor the democratic process may similarly be regarded as preventive deployment.

54. The first preventive deployment of UN troops was authorised by Security Council Resolution 795 (11 December 1992), following a request from the government of the former Yugoslav Republic of Macedonia.[4] There is now an UNPROFOR contingent of 700 troops, together with police and civilian contingents, deployed on the northern and eastern borders of Macedonia with its headquarters in Skopje. The Foreign Secretary described the UN battalion in Macedonia as a "deterrent to adventurism"[5] in the area. The FCO regarded the Macedonian deployment as "a step in the right direction".[6] On 10 June 1993 it was announced that 300 US troops would join the UN force in Macedonia. The Foreign Secretary told the Committee the USA was "very anxious to contain the war".[7]

55. Members of the Committee visited Macedonia in February, meeting members of Macedonia Command of UNPROFOR (MACCOMD) and visiting the Canadian barracks and an observation post on the border with Kosovo. We gathered that most parties in Macedonia approved of the deployment, even those who disagreed with government policy in other respects. There was some concern that, although the relevant Security Council resolution had allowed for stationing of troops in the whole country, they had in practice been deployed only on the borders with Kosovo and Albania. This was regarded by some Albanian leaders as tantamount to a suggestion that the UN expected the Albanians to invade. We were also told that there was a perception in some quarters that the UN was there to protect Macedonia in the event of attack by Serbia, and that its forces were not sufficient to do so. Nevertheless, the deployment had been generally well received, and we were impressed at the work of the UN civilian contingent in educating local opinion as to the purpose of the deployment.

---

[1] Q 365.
[2] Ev.p 188.
[3] See *An Agenda for Peace*, paras 28,31,32 and Ev.p 255.
[4] This former state of Yugoslavia was admitted as a member of the UN on 7 April 1993, under this provisional title. For the sake of brevity, it is referred to in the rest of the report as 'Macedonia'.
[5] Q 279.
[6] Ev. p 322.
[7] Ev.16 June 1993, op cit, Q 45.

56. One risk of preventive deployment of UN troops is that it may give the impression that the UN is taking sides, as distinct from the overtly impartial deployment of peacekeepers. Professor James noted that preventive deployment is far removed from "what has come to be called peace-keeping, inasmuch as it is neither impartial nor non-threatening ... the placing of a UN presence on one side only of a threatened border clearly lines up the UN on that side".[1] This kind of perception was evident in Macedonia (as mentioned in the previous paragraph). When the Committee visited Nairobi and Somalia, we learned that the Kenyan government wanted a deployment along the Somali border to prevent unrest spreading into Kenya. However, such a deployment could be interpreted as being simply a way of keeping refugees out of the country, thereby favouring the Kenyan population at the expense of displaced Somalis. The British Red Cross also expressed concern about this request.[2]

57. Another, perhaps more substantial, obstacle is that often where such a force is most needed—for instance in areas, such as on the internal boundaries within states, where civil unrest could lead to conflict—there is unlikely to be consent from all the parties involved. Lord Owen told us that ideally there would be a similar UN deployment in Kosovo to that in Macedonia but, as this would require the consent of Serbia, which was not forthcoming, it could not happen.[3] (Serbia has, however, agreed to the stationing of UNMOs at Pristina military airfield—see paragraph 53 above).

58. If the Macedonian experiment is a success—and it is far too early to predict its outcome—there will no doubt be requests from other states for similar deployments. A lightly-armed force with a limited mandate may not be enough on its own to dissuade potential aggressors. If there is a cross-border attack, larger-scale armed force may have to be used in an enforcement operation (as it was in Korea in 1950[4]). The United Nations Association suggest that, if lightly-armed forces are deployed, it should be made clear by the Security Council that action under Chapter VII would follow if a preventive deployment line were breached.[5] Dr Paul Taylor suggested that a small rapid deployment force could be kept in readiness for preventive deployment; such a force could have had a deterrent effect in Kuwait in 1990, for example.[6] Prior to deployment, a careful assessment of precisely what mandate such forces should have, and the strength in which they need to be deployed to ensure they are likely to have a sufficient deterrent effect must be carried out. However, the effectiveness of such a deployment would be increased if it could be carried out quickly, so assessment should not create too much of a delay. **We recommend that the UK as a permanent member of the Security Council support the deployment of UN missions in a preventive capacity.**

59. The Secretary-General also suggests that a traditional UN peace-keeping mechanism, the creation of **demilitarised zones**, could be employed as a preventive mechanism. Such zones could be set up at the request of one or both states in a dispute; where one side only requested it, it could serve to remove any pretext for attack.[7] Obviously the same danger applies to such an exercise as to preventive deployment—that one side will see the UN's establishment and monitoring of such a zone as taking sides. It may be that on occasion the UN wishes to take sides[8] but at an early stage in a dispute the UN might perhaps be better off maintaining its impartial and mediatory rôle. However, as with preventive deployment, **we support the concept of creating demilitarised zones as a preventive mechanism.**

60. Both preventive deployment and the preventive creation of de-militarised zones could be useful tools for the United Nations; the cost of 700 troops in Macedonia is far less than a larger-scale military operation, whether to keep the peace after a conflict or indeed to enforce a peace settlement. Obviously, the advantages of preventive deployment of troops need to be balanced against the potential risks involved: such measures could inflame a situation further unless carefully handled, and if they are to have a deterrent effect it will need to be made clear that further action may be employed by the UN if necessary. Nevertheless **we believe that the experiment in Macedonia should be seen as an encouraging precedent for similar deployments in**

---

[1] Ev.p 183.
[2] Ev.p 120.
[3] Q 190.
[4] Ev.p 183.
[5] Ev.p 269.
[6] Ev.p 185.
[7] *An Agenda for Peace*, para 33.
[8] Ev.p 183.

other potential trouble spots. As with the other preventive mechanisms of the UN, we believe that here too the acceptability and success of such operations rests on a clear understanding that behind them lie credible pressures and sanctions that can, if prevention fails, be deployed by the UN.

PEACE-KEEPING, PEACEBUILDING AND DEMOCRACY

61. Peace-keeping is not referred to in the UN Charter. It developed as a pragmatic response by the political organs to calls for the UN to contain conflicts during the Cold War. This was an era when the apparently straightforward, logical progression of UN measures to deal with disputes, threats to the peace, breaches of the peace and acts of aggression set out in Chapters VI and VII of the Charter was hampered by disputes between the permanent members about how and when the UN might act, about the authority of the Secretary-General and about the Military Staff Committee provided for in Article 47 of the Charter. Until 1987, when President Gorbachev made his historic speech to the General Assembly about the role of the UN, peace-keeping forces were generally only deployed in areas outside the direct influence of the super-powers (there were none in eastern Europe or Central America, for instance) and the troops and other personnel deployed were (apart from those in Cyprus and Lebanon) drawn from countries other than the permanent five. Some Nordic countries, Canada and India have formed the backbone of UN peace-keeping operations, and continue to play an important role.

62. Traditional UN peace-keeping operations have provided conciliatory help, using military personnel and/or civilians under the command of the United Nations, at the request of a state, states or even non-state entities (guerilla groups, liberation movements or political parties) in various types of political, diplomatic or military difficulties. Classic peace-keeping aims to calm and stabilise the situation and prevent it deteriorating; and to help to resolve the dispute, usually by supervising and verifying an agreement reached between the parties. Troops are usually lightly armed and operate under rules of engagement which allow them to use their weapons only in self defence and to protect their own positions. Soldiers serving as military observers with an observation mission or with a peace-keeping force or as military advisers are generally unarmed. A crucial pre-condition for a UN peace-keeping operation is that it has to be requested by the parties concerned: the UN cannot just decide to intervene unilaterally.

63. The different types of peace-keeping operations include predominantly military operations designed to secure and maintain a precarious ceasefire, and perhaps oversee the withdrawal of foreign troops, or verify a plan agreed between the parties. Examples of these are the United Nations Emergency Force in the Middle East in 1956 and more recently, the UN Angola Verification Mission (UNAVEM) since 1988. Such operations might include non-military activities by the UN troops as well, such as humanitarian assistance or transferring displaced citizens. Other types of peace-keeping operation have had both military and civilian components, such as in Cyprus, where soldiers and civilian police were deployed from the outset. More ambitious such operations were in Namibia, where the UN successfully monitored withdrawal of South African troops, confined the armed forces to bases and created the political conditions for and supervised free elections which led to a new constitution and to Namibia's independence. Sir David Hannay contrasted the successful Namibian operation with Cyprus which was "a bad case which has dragged on and on", though he believed the UN had saved Cyprus and its two communities from worse even if it had not brought about a solution.[1] There have also been some entirely civilian UN peace-keeping operations, such as the armed civilian guards sent by the Secretary-General to Iraq in 1991 to protect agencies supplying humanitarian assistance after the Gulf War.[2] **The success of all UN peace-keeping operations has depended crucially on the willingness of Member States to provide the cash and military resources to make them effective.**

The new generation of UN operations

64. With the end of the Cold War the UN has become involved in new geographical areas. Its activities have extended beyond the traditional Cold War areas of peace-keeping like the Middle East, Africa, the Indian subcontinent to regions where previously the permanent members' writ ran: Central America, Afghanistan, Cambodia, the former Yugoslavia and the former Soviet Union. This new generation of UN peace-keeping includes operations which have a number of special features. Operations usually have a terminal date of perhaps a year or 18

[1] Q 14.
[2] The classification of the armed civilian guards in Iraq as a "peace-keeping operation" is not universally accepted.

months, unlike that in Cyprus, for instance. Some of the new operations are very large and complex and in United Nations terms very expensive. There is usually a military element, although the emphasis is on a broad range of civilian activities: police monitoring, human rights verification, maintaining law and order, information programmes, election monitoring and conducting, constitutional advice.

65. Most significantly, **the nature of the conflicts in which the UN is being called upon to intervene has changed**—it is much more involved in intra-state, rather than inter-state, conflicts, where these are perceived to have a significant international dimension, for example if there are large numbers of displaced persons or refugees. The United Nations is more and more frequently playing an important rôle in coaxing the parties in such conflicts to a negotiated settlement and then trying to help the parties to implement that agreement. These operations are different from traditional peace-keeping where soldiers attempt to create conditions where politicians can negotiate about the underlying causes of the dispute that led to violence because the task of these new operations is to ensure that the fragile peace is stabilised.

66. Operations to try to contain or end conflicts within states (as in Somalia) or between or within new states emerging from the collapse of a state (as in Croatia, Serbia and, especially, Bosnia), where ethnic, religious or nationalist passions are high, have tended to cause the most difficulties for the UN. Witnesses stressed these problems. Professor James argued that:

> "a mission with an internal mandate can easily find itself having to act in a situation which is extremely complex and, seemingly, in perpetual motion. This is because the peacekeepers may be directly exposed to the play of politics in the jurisdiction in question ... In such a context, some of the local participants may well see the work of the peace-keeping mission as assisting their cause; others as obstructing it. They will respond accordingly."[1]

67. Another witness stressed that the UN should bear in mind "the sheer difficulty of operating in conditions of deeply engrained ethnic/communal conflict".[2] Once again, the conflict in **former Yugoslavia** is a vivid reminder of such difficulties. It is precisely this kind of conflict which the UN may be called upon more and more to try to resolve—perhaps in other states established in and around the fringes of the former Soviet Union. Sir David Hannay told us that a situation such as that in Georgia, "a kind of civil war between two factions in a post-communist situation" was very unpromising, and the UN should be cautious about becoming involved. It remains to be seen whether the recently established mission of a UN Special Representative to Georgia and Tadjikistan signals a greater willingness by the UN to become more involved in the former Soviet Union.

Peace-keeping Mandates

68. A new type of operation has emerged, using military personnel to protect the delivery of humanitarian assistance. The most obvious example of this innovation is the UNPROFOR action in **Bosnia**. The original UNPROFOR operation in **Croatia** is a more traditional peace-keeping operation, designed to "create the conditions of peace and security required for the overall settlement of the Yugoslav crisis".[3] The original mandate of British and other forces in UNPROFOR II in Bosnia was apparently clear and straightforward: to ensure the security and functioning of Sarajevo airport for the delivery of humanitarian supplies; and, operating under the leadership of UNHCR, to protect the UNHCR convoys and help them deliver humanitarian supplies to populations suffering as a consequence of conflict. The reality has proved much more complex and involves ceaseless negotiating of local ceasefires, securing the agreement of warring groups which often operate without reference to their supposed political leaders, for bridges to be rebuilt to allow the convoys through, and coping with the appalling and distressing consequences of "ethnic cleansing".

69. The mandate of UNPROFOR troops in Bosnia was extended on 4 June 1993 to enable it, under Chapter VII of the Charter, in the safe areas for some of the Muslim population designated in a previous resolution, "to deter attacks against the safe areas, to monitor the ceasefire, to promote the withdrawal of military or paramilitary units other than those of the government of the republic of Bosnia and Herzogovina and to occupy some key points on the

---

[1] Ev.pp 181–82.
[2] Professor Roberts, Ev.p 314.
[3] SCR 743. February 1992.

ground, in addition to participating in the delivery of humanitarian relief". UNPROFOR was also mandated under this resolution "to take the necessary measures, including the use of force, in reply to bombardments against the safe areas... or to armed incursion into them or in the event of any deliberate obstruction in or around those areas to the freedom of movement of UNPROFOR or of protecting humanitarian convoys."[1] Thus an enforcement mandate has been bolted on to the previous mandate of UNPROFOR in Bosnia. UNPROFOR's ability to exercise this new mandate will depend on the willingness of states to contribute troops, equipment, logistics and finance.

70. There are good reasons why UN troops, even when mandated to use force if they are obstructed by factions on the ground, do so only rarely. The United Nations needs to maintain its impartiality even though the effects of its activities might be regarded by one of the parties as partial;[2] it needs the continued cooperation of the parties if it is to be successful no matter how frustrating the barriers put in its way to prevent peace-keeping troops quickly executing their mission; the troops are not equipped to fight their way through—they have been armed on the expectation that the parties will honour their commitments—therefore their wisest choice is to negotiate their way through. No doubt United Nations troops might be able to destroy the first roadblock they encounter, or deal with the first threatening soldiers or irregulars they meet, but thereafter they are likely to become the target of violence which will not only prevent them from fulfilling their mission but would also increase their casualties. Therefore they learn to muddle through in messy situations where there are irresponsible violent groups who appear not to accept any national leadership. Recent experience in Bosnia and in Somalia suggests that encounters with armed groups who are not vulnerable to the normal state pressures which induce agreement, who appear not to worry about their inconsistent behaviour, their duplicity, their honour or their reputation seem likely to become increasingly common in internal peace-keeping operations. So agreements have to be negotiated, and if necessary renegotiated, locally for virtually every convoy of assistance.

71. The largest example so far of a combined military and civilian operation is in **Cambodia**, where UNTAC, the UN transitional authority, has acted almost as a transitional sovereign authority until the election of a new government. Under their mandate UN troops in Cambodia cannot intervene to stop outbreaks of fighting between the several armies maintained by the parties in Cambodia: "peace-keeping" there has amounted to patrols when it is safe for troops to patrol, staying in barracks when fighting breaks out and then reporting on the incidents which breach the ceasefire in an attempt to shame the parties into stopping the skirmishes. The disregarding by all parties to the agreement, especially the Khmer Rouge, of the ceasefire agreed in Paris and widespread harassment by all parties of their political opponents during the election campaign, illustrated the ultimate inability of a UN peace-keeping operation to keep the peace if the parties themselves do not keep their word. This is frustrating and at times dangerous for the UN personnel (military and civilian) concerned and threatens the credibility of the UN as a whole. It also led to calls for the UN to *enforce* the peace agreement.

72. Another complex operation is the so far apparently successful one in **El Salvador**. This, one of the most intrusive UN operations in terms of state sovereignty, was deployed while the civil war continued. This was remarkable because such operations have in the past usually begun only when a ceasefire is in place. What was even more remarkable in that case was that the UN staff in the human rights division of the operation went to El Salvador without military protection despite receiving serious threats to their lives.

73. In **Somalia** it is worth remembering that the deployment of UNITAF and UNOSOM II forces has not covered the northern area, primarily the former British Somaliland where the conflict did not wholly destry order, and where there is a real chance of building upon long-standing local power structures. The United Nations claimed that the original UNOSOM operation failed not because of inadequate rules of engagement but primarily because there was an absence of recognised political authorities with whom the organisation could reliably conclude agreements for the deployment and activities of the peacekeepers, and because the war lords in different parts of Somalia were not willing, or in some cases able, to provide the cooperation for the United Nations to succeed.[3] Once this had been realised the Security Council endorsed

---

[1] SCR 836, June 1993.
[2] Ev.p 183, Q 398 (Professor James).
[3] See Q 9.

the Secretary-General's recommendation that an enforcement mandate be provided to Member States led by the United States who formed the Unified Task Force (UNITAF), later replaced by UNOSOM II, a UN force with similar mandate and rules of engagement.[1] The killing on 5 June 1993 of large numbers of Pakistani UN troops in UNOSOM II and subsequent events provide a graphic illustration of the dangers inherent in such a peace enforcement operation and indicate how the UN may be entering a complex and difficult military commitment there.

Elections

74. The United Nations has been involved in varying degrees with elections. In some countries this has consisted of observing elections. In **Nicaragua** in 1989/90 the Secretary-General sent several missions before the election was held to observe the revision of the electoral laws and the laws governing the mass media and to study the resultant legislation. Although the United Nations had been asked only to observe the election it established a parallel voting system which allowed it to be the first observer group, by many hours, to predict accurately the result. This information was used by the Secretary-General's personal representative, Mr Elliott Richardson, in the process of persuading the President of Nicaragua to accept the totally unexpected result and the victorious parties to behave magnanimously. A UN Election Observation Mission was sent to **Haiti** in October 1990 to observe the presidential elections; this included some military personnel who advised the Haitian armed forces on a security plan for the elections and monitored the implementation of the plan. President Aristide, elected in December 1990, was subsequently overthrown in September 1991. Negotiations are continuing to try to restore democracy in Haiti. In **South Africa** the UN is involved at a stage prior to elections, with the sending in 1993 of UN observers to monitor the democractic process.

75. The next level of electoral operation has been to observe and verify elections. In 1991–92 in **Angola** the United Nations monitored and evaluated the operation and the impartiality of the electoral authorities as they registered voters, organised the poll, conducted the elections, counted the votes and announced the result. The mission also viewed important political rallies and other political activities and verified compliance by all the parties with the electoral law and the code of conduct. UNITA'S refusal to recognise the result of that election has been followed by a resumption of fighting in Angola. In **Eritrea** the UN provided initial assistance with and observers during the referendum in 1993 on Eritrean secession from Ethiopia: the first time the UN has assisted with the amicable division of a state in this manner.

76. A third level of UN involvement has been the supervision and control of an election. In **Namibia**, for instance, every part of the election process including electoral legislation, voter registration and the conduct of the poll by the South African Administrator-General had to receive the imprimatur of the Personal Representative of the Secretary-General. The work of UNTAG in Namibia where the UN-supervised free election helped bring about an independent Namibia has since been cited as a model for future UN operations.[2]

77. The final level has been for the United Nations actually to organise and conduct the total election process itself. In **Western Sahara** the United Nations is supposed to be conducting a referendum to determine whether the inhabitants wish to see the territory merge with Morocco or to become an independent state. Disagreement over who should be eligible to vote, however, has prevented any further implementation of the peace plan. In **Cambodia** where the United Nations was charged with attempting to create a politically neutral environment in which it could organise elections for the choosing of a new government and the creation of a new constitution, one of the successes of the operation was the registration of 4.7 million electors including tens of thousands of people whom the UN had helped to repatriate from neighbouring countries, particularly Thailand. The election, however was held against a backdrop of possible violence because the Khmer Rouge refused to have 70% of its soldiers cantoned, disarmed and demobilised. In the event the election passed off peaceably and the result suggests that the UN in Cambodia succeeded in keeping down levels of political intimidation and enabled the people to exercise free choice. The UN Transitional Authority has declared FUNCIPEC the winner and that the election was free and fair. The way in which a new government will be formed in Cambodia and the rôle of Prince Sihanouk, however, remain obscure at the time of

---

[1] Marrack Goulding: The evolution of UN Peacekeeping, op cit, p 10.
[2] Q 14, Ev.p 260.

writing but it brings the democratic process into disrepute if the Khmer Rouge, who opted out of the election, were invited to participate in the formation of a government.

Disarming the parties

78. Peace-keeping forces can be called upon to disarm and demobilise troops as part of their mandate. Sometimes such disarmament follows ceasefires negotiated after the deployment of peace-keeping forces—as in the Muslim enclave of Srebrenica in **Bosnia**. This has led to the grim irony of UN troops taking surrender of Muslim weapons at the same time as the area was under attack by Bosnian Serb forces. The mandate of ONUCA in **Central America**, was extended and armed infantry joined their unarmed military observer colleagues, first in Honduras to demobilize and destroy the weapons of the Nicaraguan resistance, and then in Nicaragua to monitor an internal ceasefire, separate governmental and Contra forces and then to demobilize the resistance. In other cases, the original agreement under which peace-keeping troops are deployed includes provision for them to oversee disarming and demobilisation of armies as part of an overall peace agreement between the parties.

79. Part of the mandate of UNAVEM in **Angola** was to verify that the joint monitoring groups, composed in equal numbers of representatives of UNITA and the MPLA-led government, were undertaking their responsibilities. Those responsibilities included ensuring that the ceasefire was maintained and that the troops were gathered at their collecting point. The UN mission also provided advice to the two parties on the assembly and the demobilisation of troops and the custody of their weapons. It would appear that UNITA did not disarm according to the peace accords and thus was able to resume fighting after it refused to accept the results of the internationally observed election. The operation in Angola can be seen to have failed in the sense that one of the parties refused to accept the result of the ballot box and was able to return to fighting because it appeared that it had not demobilized according to the agreement. The United Nations, however, did not withdraw and sought to broker a ceasefire, attempted to contain the violence and persuade the parties to return to the negotiating process. The mission has been reduced in size but the Secretary-General has retained the option of increasing it should that be thought desirable and useful.

80. One of the tasks of the military components of UNTAC in **Cambodia** was the supervision of the ceasefire, and the regroupment, cantonment, disarming and demobilisation of 70% of the forces of the four factions. The decision of the Khmer Rouge not to comply with this key provision has affected the implementation of the Paris Accords and affected every aspect of the UNTAC operation. The Security Council, however, decided to proceed with the election even though it would be difficult to guarantee the main purpose of the operation: a politically neutral environment in which the electorate of Cambodia could choose freely their new government. In **Somalia**, the extent to which UNOSOM II can enforce the disarmament of the factional leaders will be critical for the success of the reconstruction of the country. The United Nations has bombed the headquarters of one of the warring factions following its lack of cooperation with the disarmament process.

Police

81. Two recent UN operations have included substantial components of civilian police. In **El Salvador** the purposes of the United Nations civil police were to ensure that the National Police Force did not violate human rights, that it acted impartially and thus helped to create confidence in national reconciliation. But here again the United Nations faced difficulties:

— The full strength of the police division was intended to be 693. This was reduced by the Secretariat to 362, yet in March 1992 only 264 policemen had been deployed because Member States were unable to provide sufficient personnel.

— The United Nations civil police were monitoring a national police force that appeared to be unable to maintain law and order. For example, the national force was asked to uphold property laws in the countryside the legitimacy of which was challenged; it was poorly equipped and trained; its morale was low because of uncertainty about its future (according to the peace agreements a new national police force was to be established); and the national force had no presence in the areas controlled by the liberation movement.

— The United Nations police force did not have enough personnel to monitor adequately police activities in every town where there was a police presence. It could not operate at night. And it could not at the outset provide security in the FMLN (liberation front) zones because its mandate initially only covered the activities of the national police force.[1]

82. In Cambodia the United Nations civil police were meant to play a very important rôle in helping to ensure a neutral political environment for the elections by supervising or controlling the local police of the four political factions. During the visit to Cambodia, members of the Committee were told that the civilian police were the weakest link in the UNTAC operation. This weakness was attributed to a variety of factors. The first was lack of preparation for the police operation:

— The UN Police Commissioner was not formally appointed until the first week of March 1992 and arrived in Cambodia two weeks later.

— There was insufficient time for serious planning or for establishing standard operating procedures before the deployment of the police.

— Officers had come from 30 forces with varying standards and different training: when police arrived they did not know what their task was or what their powers were.

— There were communications problems. All police should have been able to speak either French or English, but English-speaking police officers were unable to communicate with the French-speaking ones and between 10% and 20% of the UN police officers did not speak either language with sufficient fluency.

83. Secondly, United Nations police did not have formal powers of arrest although the Special Prosecutor's Office established by UNTAC in Phnom Penh could issue orders to arrest violators of the law especially human rights violations. Thirdly, the United Nations police found it very difficult indeed to maintain the peace:

— It was very difficult to monitor the local police, who had had no police training and very poor equipment.

— There were no criminal or traffic laws.

— Local police salaries were very low and some were not paid at all. We were told that the police were corrupt: they established illegal checkpoints, demanded protection money, stopped vehicles and took bribes. And reports to the Interior Ministry were not acted upon.

— The police and the UNTAC Human Rights component found it very difficult to investigate human rights violations because many were committed by soldiers and there were insurmountable difficulties in investigating military units.

— The local authorities were attempting to interfere with the election process by trying to collect UN Identity Cards which contained photographs from village people. This psychological harassment was very widespread and very difficult to prevent.

84. An Australian diplomat based in Phnom Penh, Mr Nick Warner, has suggested that the Police Planning Unit in the UN Secretariat in New York should establish basic standard operating procedures for the police for future peace-keeping operations. He also believes that the police needed to be trained for United Nations service. There were many different police methods in use around the world. A standard training was required.[2]

Other novel aspects of the Cambodian operation

85. Mr Warner's paper described three areas in which the peace-keeping operation in Cambodia has broken new ground. The first is UHNCR's repatriation programme which has been an outstanding success. For the first time in UNHCR's history a field operation has been totally managed from the field, with the delegation of authority and financial arrangements to Phnom Penh. As a result, UNHCR has been flexible in planning and in execution and in responding to changing situations. Whatever happens in Cambodia after the election in May 1993, the achievement of the UNHCR operation to repatriate over 350,000 refugees from

---

[1] Stephen Baranyi and Liisa North, Stretching the limits of the Possible: United Nations Peacekeeping in Central America. Aurora Papers 15 Canadian Centre for Global Security, Ottawa, Ontario, Canada 1992 pp 30–32.
[2] Cambodia: Lessons of UNTAC for future peacekeeping operations, Mr Nick Warner. Paper given at an International Seminar, Canberra, March 1993.

camps in Thailand was remarkable. Committee members who visited Cambodia saw some of the last refugees returning from the Khao-i-Dang camp to begin a new life and were deeply impressed by all aspects of the operation, and by the UNHCR personnel they met.

86. The second area where the Cambodia operation broke new ground was UNTAC's direct control of the police and five civil administration areas: defence, information, public security, foreign affairs and finance in order to establish a neutral political environment. Mr Warner believes that more in-depth planning and consideration of the concept and the requirement of direct control before the deployment of UNTAC would have been advantageous.[1] Nothing as intrusive as the direct control function has ever been attempted by the United Nations before. To achieve a neutral political environment through the control of only these areas of government, as compared with full executive and legislative powers, would have been difficult in any polity. But this has been even more so in Cambodia where there were ostensibly four separate administrative elements and police forces to control, little workable infrastructure and serious language problems.

87. The third novel aspect of the Cambodia operation has been UNTAC's tentative moves to establish an independent judicial system. In early 1993 a Special Prosecutor's Office was established. The Special Representative (Mr Akashi) also authorised UNTAC police and military officers to arrest and detain those suspected of involvement in acts of political violence. These decisions were taken by Mr Akashi after an alarming increase in attacks on political party officers and officials in November and December and the inadequate response by the relevant administrative authority. These unplanned but legitimate actions verge on enforcement by the UN because the United Nations civil police were given, for the first time in a UN operation, the power of arrest. They also raise the question as to whether UN police should be armed in future operations.

Trusteeship

88. The growth of the UN's work in tackling huge mandates such as in Cambodia and Somalia has been accompanied by calls for the UN to start taking on the administration of entire countries where government has broken down. The term "trusteeship" is sometimes used. Is the UN actually capable of taking on the administration of countries and if so, would this be a good idea? It could well be seen as neo-colonialism. The Foreign Secretary has used the word "imperial" in discussing the UN's new rôle, although he emphasized to us that this was a deliberate attempt to provoke debate about the way in which the UN was taking on far larger mandates than ever before.[2] Professor James told us that the UN was nothing like a "world government" and that the "imperial" remark was "disturbing". He believed Member States would be very concerned if they thought the UN were to expand its peace-keeping operation into "taking over" countries.[3] There was a difference between the UN going into a country as part of an agreement with the parties (as was the case in Cambodia) and unilaterally deciding to go into a country and run it.[4] Professor Higgins was equally cautious about the "imperial rôle", although she agreed that in very exceptional cases, and on a short term basis, the UN might have to step in and run a state or territory (as in the case of West Irian).[5] Dr Taylor stressed the need for the UN's aim to be to rebuild local structures rather than "acting as a trustee and moving in".[6]

89. There has been some discussion recently of reviving "UN trusteeship" in the case of states which are deemed no longer to be able to govern themselves. It is worth recalling exactly what the Charter says about this, and how far it differs from more recent ideas about the UN administering states. Under Chapter XII of the UN Charter, provision is made for non-self governing territories to be placed under the trusteeship of a Member State (the administering authority). The aim of the trusteeship system was to promote the advancement of the population of the trust territories and their progressive development towards self-government or independence. Essentially the system was designed to allow individual Member States to act as trustees of territories within a UN framework, their relationship being supervised by the Trusteeship Council. The last remaining trust territory, Palau, is administered by the USA.

---

[1] *Ibid.*
[2] Ev.p 245.
[3] Ev.p 181.
[4] Q 406.
[5] Q 406.
[6] Q 404.

Under article 78 of the Charter, no Member State can become a trust territory. Were a state like Somalia or Bosnia to become a trust territory within the strict meaning of the Charter, it would first have to renounce its membership of the UN.

Peace-keeping: an assessment

90. The Security Council appears to be facing a ceaseless demand for United Nations assistance. The Council finds it difficult to say no because it fears that some states might relapse into internal violence with implications for international peace or that some states might even disappear without immediate succour. However, **the Security Council must ensure that peace-keeping operations are not deployed unless there is a reasonable chance of success. It may be necessary for the Council to resist demands, demonstrate that conditions are not propitious and insist that some other method than peace-keeping should be used.**

91. Another factor which should be borne in mind is that, **once UN military forces are present they are liable to be used in a range of ways. Contributing states will always insist that the remit for their forces is laid down in precise terms. But while this might be possible *initially*, once on the ground there will be pressures for their rôle to be extended.**

92. The nature of peace-keeping operations has evolved rapidly in recent years and principles and practice have responded flexibly to new demands. According to the Secretary-General "the basic conditions for success remain unchanged". They include: a clear and practicable mandate; the cooperation of the parties in implementing that mandate; and the continuing support of the Security Council.[1] **Any successful UN operation must have a practicable mandate and the support of the Security Council; where there is no cooperation from the parties to the conflict, the UN must decide whether it wishes to attempt to impose its solutions on the situation. Peace-keeping is a consent-based, impartial activity; enforcement is not. We believe that there must be a clear distinction between the two activities and that there are grave difficulties in combining them in a given location.**

93. The use of troops in peace-keeping operations falls within the second category of UN operation described in para 22 above: they are impartial military operations, extensions of diplomacy using military expertise; they are not direct military action by the UN. If the parties concerned respect agreements UN forces can perform important tasks which go beyond simply policing ceasefires or patrolling borders. If the political agreements are broken, traditional, lightly armed peacekeepers may not be able to keep the peace.

94. **We consider that calls for military deployment on the ground to enforce in Bosnia a disputed peace plan have been misconceived: troops equipped for peace-keeping or humanitarian protection work cannot be transformed into a UN fighting force simply by passing a new Security Council resolution. Security Council Resolution 836 extended the mandate of UNPROFOR to enable it to deter attacks against the safe areas and to begin to implement part of the Vance-Owen plan.[2] We are not persuaded that it is practicable to try to impose a peace plan in Bosnia from outside. We fear that attempting so to impose a plan for the constitutional structure of part of former Yugoslavia could make things worse rather than better for the civilian population as well as having serious consequences for the safety of UN personnel there, which includes a large British contingent, and for the future willingness of governments to allow UN peacekeepers into their states.[3] It may also affect governments' willingness to contribute troops to UN operations in the future.**

95. **Experience of recent peace-keeping operations, and in particular the experiences in Bosnia and Cambodia lead us to the conclusion that the Security Council must be persuaded to recognise that not all proposals for peace-keeping operations can be put into effect successfully. We urge the United Kingdom to use its influence in the Security Council to ensure that peace-keeping operations, particularly on the scale of these recent operations, are entered into only when there is a realistic prospect of their objectives being achieved. Where the UN does decide to intervene, we recommend that the mandates laid down for UN military and civilian operations be rigorously scrutinised to try to ensure their practicability and that no commitment to a peace-keeping operation be entered into by the Security Council unless there is a firm prospect of the necessary**

---

[1] *An Agenda for Peace*, para 50.
[2] SCR 836.
[3] See Q 387.

resources—human and financial—being available from the Member States to allow the operation a realistic chance of being fully implemented.

96. The Secretary-General is finding increasing difficulty in mounting peace-keeping operations quickly. First, while the demand for peace-keeping increases many states are reducing the size of their armed forces and although the Secretary-General has broadened the range of states providing personnel to sixty-seven he is still faced with the challenge of finding militarily efficient troops who are acceptable to the parties. Furthermore some governments are becoming wary of long-term commitments to operations in which a settlement to the underlying problem is still being sought as in the former Yugoslavia or Cyprus, and they worry whether the mandate may shift under the pressure of events, leading to unacceptable casualties. The Secretary-General has always faced problems in recruiting logistics units, which few governments are willing to release, and he has found civilian police hard to obtain.

97. Secondly, financial constraints have affected the speed of mounting and deploying an operation. The United Nations is almost always in a cash flow problem because of the deficits on the regular and peace-keeping budgets. There is often a gap between the authorization of an operation by the Security Council and the approval of the budget by the General Assembly. The cost of peace-keeping has risen very sharply because of the increase in the number of operations, particularly the complex multifunctional operations that involve large numbers of civilians. These are employed at salaries greatly in excess of the allowance of $15,000 per annum per solider, regardless of rank, that the United Nations pays to the contributing states. The new peace-keeping reserve fund, which became operational in February 1993 may, providing it is regularly replenished, mitigate to some degree the financial problems of quickly deploying a force. This and other aspects of paying for peace-keeping are discussed in more detail in section VI below.

HUMANITARIAN INTERVENTION AND ASSISTANCE

98. Perhaps the most complex and difficult problem with which the UN is currently grappling is this: under what circumstances is humanitarian intervention by the international community justified? The number and diversity of humanitarian crises have increased sharply over the past few years and enhanced media coverage has heightened public awareness of the suffering involved and increased expectations of the ability of governments and of the UN to respond. Not only are there more concurrent crises, they are becoming more complex, with civil conflict inextricably linked with the need for humanitarian assistance.[1] The pattern of recent experiences is that even the most 'internal' of issues tends to have international repercussions, most immediately because of the pressures on neighbouring states caused by floods of refugees across borders. There is no consensus as to whether there exists a right to intervene in a sovereign state without the consent of its government in order to alleviate human suffering. The issue straddles many of the other aspects of UN intervention discussed in this Report. **Humanitarian intervention does not always inevitably involve use of the military. Military intervention for humanitarian purposes is a new phenomenon for the United Nations. It has happened to protect aid convoys (as in former Yugoslavia), distribute food directly (as in military air lifts to Sarajevo and other parts of Bosnia and Somalia), to protect areas designated as safe havens or safe areas (as in Iraq and now in Bosnia) and to help to rebuild a civil society (as in Somalia).**

99. Recently, with the end of the Cold War, there has been a revival of the call for an absolute right of intervention. Some French campaigners have pressed for a "*droit d'ingerence*" or right to intervene to provide relief.[2] In 1988 and 1990 the General Assembly passed, on French initiative, resolutions on humanitarian assistance "to victims of natural disasters and similar emergency situations". They did not cover non-natural or political disasters. As the Development Studies Association pointed out, these resolutions also reaffirmed the sovereignty of the States affected.[3] Sir David Hannay told us that there had been a "big shift" in the last two or three years away from what had previously been the accepted wisdom: that there would be no intervention in the internal affairs of states. This had come about "by a kind of organic process, an evolution of opinion" and Sir David told us that some Members of the Security Council had been surprised when non-aligned African States had called for UN troops to be put into Somalia to protect the aid effort. He argued, however, that a pragmatic, organic

---

[1] Ev.pp 27,35,115,116,149; Q 313.
[2] Ev.p 295. Q 15.
[3] See Ev.p 295.

approach was needed to proposals for humanitarian intervention and that there would be fundamental objections to any attempt to rewrite the UN Charter explicitly to permit intervention in matters within the domestic jurisdiction of states.[1]

100. The British Red Cross argued that a right to intervene, the "so-called *droit d'ingerence*", was doubtful law. It also pointed out that it could have undesired side-effects: "No one wishes to have the United States, for example, intervene in Northern Ireland".[2] It argued that using force to aid victims of conflict was not an acceptable alternative to addressing the root cause of a conflict. The Red Cross believed the UN was at its most useful when it provided a forum for the resolution of conflict, "since conflict may itself be the source of humanitarian emergency" and cited examples in Nicaragua, El Salvador, Cambodia, Sri Lanka, Afghanistan and former Yugoslavia.[3] During the Cold War, any attempt to get agreement between the permanent members of the Security Council, let alone the non-aligned members of the UN, that the UN had any right to intervene in internal disputes was unthinkable. In the case of Somalia, the former UN Special Representative, Ambassador Sahnoun, described to us the length of time it took to convince the UN to intervene.[4] We were told in New York that when the Security Council did eventually decide to do so, it had been considered necessary to obtain a formal but essentially artificial request for it to do so.[5]

101. The two most significant recent examples of humanitarian intervention are the operation in **Iraq** to provide assistance and protection to Iraq's Shias and Kurds after the Gulf War and the vast, originally US-led operation in Somalia, which now includes troops from many different countries. The operation in Somalia, where military intervention was accompanied by civilian officials who went in first to seek the cooperation of Elders and women's groups, quickly and dramatically achieved its original purpose of bringing food to people who were starving in that country. In the case of Iraq, according to the Red Cross, aid for the victims was an "essential corollary" of Security Council action against an aggressor.[6] Their witness stressed, however, that these were "very special circumstances".[7] Foreign Office officials told us that Operation Provide Comfort was:

> "not specifically mandated by the United Nations, but the states taking action in northern Iraq did so in exercise of the customary international law principle of humanitarian intervention."[8]

102. Mr Anthony Aust, legal Counsellor in the FCO, described four criteria which might be used by the international community to decide whether to intervene on humanitarian grounds. These were:

— whether there was a compelling and urgent situation of extreme humanitarian distress which demanded immediate relief;

— whether the state in question was itself able or willing to meet that distress and deal with it;

— whether there was any other practical alternative to intervening to relieve the distress; and

— whether the action could be limited in time and scope.[9]

The Development Studies Association (DSA) proposed a similar list of criteria to apply where military force is required for non-consensual intervention.[10]

103. Mr Aust explained the device used by the Security Council to enable it to intervene on humanitarian grounds. Article 2.7 of the Charter prohibits intervention in matters "essentially" within the domestic jurisdiction of states; and its provisions are without prejudice to the appli-

---

[1] Q 11.
[2] Ev.p 118.
[3] *Ibid.*
[4] Qs 419–421.
[5] See SCR 733 and Ev.p 296.
[6] Ev.p 118.
[7] Q 229.
[8] Q 109.
[9] Q 142.
[10] Ev.p 298.

cation of enforcement measures under Chapter VII of the Charter. Mr Aust told us, "humanitarian matters are, of course, now matters of international concern". Where the Security Council decides that suffering poses a threat to international peace and security, as required under Chapter VII, it can override Article 2.7 and intervene. It is a political matter. Sir Crispin Tickell described this as a "device",[1] Professor Higgins as a "technique".[2] The question then is: at what point will the Security Council make a determination that a humanitarian crisis poses a threat to international peace and security?

104. One reason for trying to lay down clear rules about the circumstances in which the UN can intervene to provide humanitarian relief, and the circumstances in which it cannot so act, is to stop such action being, as now, selective. Ad hoc decisions to intervene run the risk of incurring accusations of neocolonialism by the big powers in the Security Council.

105. Mr Olara Otunnu, President of the International Peace Academy in New York, identified two schools of thought: one, based largely in the northern countries of the world, "wants to see a more elastic interpretation of non-interference ... some watering down of national sovereignty at least with regard to the issue of humanitarian emergencies and disasters". The other he described as "the status quo school, that is deeply concerned about any erosion of the barriers erected by non-interference", who were mainly developing countries. Although he sensed a mood of "gradual erosion of national sovereignty" across the world, "in fact, if not in juridical terms" Mr Otunnu thought an ad hoc, case by case approach was inevitable.[3] Mr Hogg believed it was quite impossible to codify the circumstances in which the UN could intervene.[4] The Foreign Secretary asked the Committee's help in trying "to set out some sort of guidelines as to when we say yes and when we say no".[5]

106. Our predecessor Committee concluded that "it is better to make law gradually for the UN by means of particular cases, rather than dismantle Article 2.7. Indeed, the case law relating to Iraq establishes important precedents for the UN in the future".[6] Professor Higgins and Sir John Thomson thought that a "piecemeal" approach should be adopted in regard to developing a case law of intervention.[7]

107. The current discussion about the *droit d'ingerence* assumes that the international community has to some extent accepted the premise. However, is this actually the case? The most-cited example of direct intervention against the will of the government for humanitarian purposes is **Iraq**, but as various witnesses pointed out, that intervention was within a defeated country negotiating from a position of weakness. **Somalia** was a country with no government at all—the UNITAF deployment was not carried out against the wishes of the authorities but in their absence. Neither can be regarded as a satisfactory precedent or model for further intervention.

108. A better test case might be a country like **Sudan**, where there is extreme hardship and internal conflict, but also an authoritarian government which is highly suspicious of outside intervention even when it is purely humanitarian.[8] Mr Otunnu suggested that in **Kosovo** too it was possible that, should a major emergency develop there, with the state structures remaining in place, the international community might feel that the state was not attending sufficiently to an emergency within its borders.[9] Humanitarian intervention in **Bosnia** may now have reached the point where the question of the state's acquiescence in the international humanitarian relief effort is no longer relevant. Whether the various parties to the conflict continue to like it or not, the international community is unlikely to withdraw from its humanitarian relief effort.

109. The DSA noted that the question of intervention by force and the provision of humanitarian relief are not discrete subjects.[10] This is illustrated by the problems associated with a military component to the delivery of aid as in Somalia or Bosnia. Providing humanitarian

---

[1] Q 380.
[2] Ev.p 179.
[3] Olara Otunnu, 'Emerging Trends in the New World Situation', The Round Table (1992), 324 (401–409).
[4] Q 110.
[5] Q 270.
[6] The Middle East after the Gulf War, Third Report from the Foreign Affairs Committee, HC 143(1990–91) para 7.11.
[7] Ev.p 179, Q 380.
[8] Cf QQ 85–89; see also Ev.p 31.
[9] Otunnu, op cit.
[10] Ev.p 297.

relief can be seen as a political act whether accompanied by a military presence or not.[1] All intervention, including humanitarian intervention, and most especially intervention by military means, must be seen to be supported not simply by the permanent five but by the UN as a whole. Continuing efforts need to be made to ensure that UN operations retain the backing of the international community as a whole.

110. **The old constraints embodied in Article 2.7 of the Charter against interference in matters which are "essentially" domestic are no longer accepted. The change is a very recent one and has occurred in response to two very different emergencies: in Somalia and in Iraq after the Gulf War. Decisions to intervene militarily on humanitarian grounds have not been taken according to a clear set of guiding principles, but in response to sudden emergencies. The UN has not so intervened in other humanitarian disasters of perhaps comparable scale—such as that in Sudan. Better criteria, which are internationally accepted, need to be drawn up to determine the circumstances in which armed intervention for humanitarian purposes is acceptable. The criteria listed in paragraph 102 above may form a good basis on which to build. In the end, however, the decision on whether actually to intervene militarily for humanitarian purposes will depend on each occasion on the exact circumstances of the emergency in question.**

HUMAN RIGHTS WORK

111. Article 1.3 of the UN Charter states that one of the organisation's aims is "promoting and encouraging respect for human rights and for fundamental freedoms for all". *An Agenda for Peace* mentions human rights only in passing (para 3), but the denial of human rights on a large scale can be a destabilising factor for international security.[2] Professor Higgins's evidence[3] contains a useful summary of the various organs through which the UN attempts to fulfil these aims, and the FCO has submitted evidence on the UK's contributions to them.[4]

112. Human rights form a major part of the UN's reconstruction and reconciliation work. The UN has done remarkable work in the field of human rights in many parts of the world. For instance, the Truth Commission in **El Salvador** has been granted extensive powers to examine allegations of human rights abuse and has exposed a number of highly placed politicians. The human rights component of UNTAC in **Cambodia** has an extensive programme of work, reflecting the declared aim of the Paris Agreement to assure protection of human rights and implementing a programme of human rights education. In the **former Yugoslavia**, the CSCE is undertaking valuable human rights monitoring in liaison with the UN and this will be even more important whatever settlement is finally reached.

113. Witnesses suggested that the capacity of the UN institutions established to fulfil the aims of the Charter in respect of human rights was far from satisfactory. Professor Higgins, who is a member of the UN Committee on Human Rights, stated bluntly that the United Nations Centre for Human Rights in Geneva, which services the various UN treaty bodies and other organs devoted to human rights, is "extremely under resourced ... [it] is not only short of staff. It lacks the most basic amenities including word processors and a fax machine".[5] This is despite an ever-increasing workload.[6] Professor Higgins suggested that "moribund subsidiary organs", such as the various regional economic commissions or the Council for Namibia[7] could be abolished and the money saved spent on the human rights centre.

114. The Government agrees that the human rights programme is operating "under severe strain".[8] The Government is pressing for increased resources to be made available to the human rights programme—in particular to the UN Centre for Human Rights—within existing UN budgetary constraints,[9] and the EC has made representations to the Secretary-General to find more staff for the Human Rights Commission in Geneva.[10] Presumably any extra money will come either from greater efficiency, the abolition of other programmes or organs (as sug-

---

[1] Q 388, Ev.p 188.
[2] Ev.p 180.
[3] Ev.pp 180–81.
[4] Ev.p 59.
[5] Ev.p 180.
[6] *Ibid.*
[7] Q 409.
[8] Ev.p 59.
[9] Ev.p 59.
[10] Q 22.

gested by Professor Higgins) or both. **The FCO stated that the Government was keen for the UN to play a more prominent rôle in the field of human rights, and sought to improve the implementation of the existing human rights instruments and to assist states to fulfil their international obligations in this field, as well as supporting increased funding for the human rights organs of the UN.[1] We support these aims.**

115. We broadly agree with Professor Higgins's strictures on the underfunding of the UN's human rights apparatus. Issues of funding, staffing and resources must be addressed. Member States, who subscribe to the principles of the UN Charter, must demonstrate the political will to implement them, as without political impetus the work of the UN in the field of human rights will continue to be underfunded and undervalued. **The Government should support the abolition or rationalisation of UN organs that have outlived their usefulness if this is necessary to release resources for the UN's human rights work.**

116. The government has also said that it is considering how best to contribute to the trust fund set up by the UN Human Rights Commission to provide for its future requirements.[2] Respect for human rights is "an intrinsic part of the UK's good government policy, as well as an objective of British foreign policy in its own right ... good government [including promotion of individual rights and access to equitable laws] remains a central concern of the aid programme".[3] **We recommend that the Government, given its long-standing commitment to human rights, make a substantial contribution to the UN's human rights Trust Fund. Compatibility should be ensured between the government's actions within the UN and its "good government" decisions.**

117. One of the most significant triggers for internal conflict is unrest centred on ethnic or national minorities within states. The question of extending to such minorities the human rights protection enjoyed—at least in theory—by individuals was discussed at the last session of the UN General Assembly, which agreed a Declaration on the Rights of Persons belonging to National or Ethnic, Religious and Linguistic Minorities. This declaration is not a mandatory instrument and it remains to be seen how far Member States will implement its provisions in practice. But the same question remains for this undertaking as for questions of human rights more generally: is the international community satisfied merely to agree forms of words which it does not have the means—or the will—to enforce?

118. **Debate at the World Conference on Human Rights in Vienna in June 1993 demonstrated that maintaining international consensus on definitions of human rights, let alone whether to enforce such rights is not practicable.** Gross violations of human rights are a breach of international humanitarian law.[4] Professor Rosalyn Higgins told us that it was generally agreed that violations of human rights were not matters of domestic concern only. The important question was not whether the UN *could* intervene in such circumstances but whether the UN could engage in enforcement measures.[5] She stressed the importance, if the UN does move towards enforcing human rights through the Security Council, that it should be seen to be done even-handedly.[6] She pointed out that in former Yugoslavia there had been major human rights violations, so intervention by the UN on the grounds that these constituted a threat to international peace and security was permissible. The question of whether actually to intervene was one of political judgement.[7] **As with intervention on other humanitarian grounds, decisions on whether to intervene on human rights grounds will always be exceptionally delicate ones for the UN to contemplate and can only be decided on a pragmatic, case by case, basis. Nevertheless, the UN must always be conscious of its responsibility to act and to be seen to be acting in a consistent and even-handed way.**

119. **The exposure of massive human rights abuses is a proper rôle of the UN and we support the Secretary-General's proposal referred to in paragraph 45 above that such violations be brought to the attention of the Security Council. We recommend that the Government press for**

---

[1] Ev.p 59.
[2] Official Report 26 March 1993 c 748W.
[3] FCO Departmental Report 1993, Cm 2202 pp 15, 42, 45.
[4] Ev.p 179 and Q 386.
[5] Ev.p 179.
[6] Q 386.
[7] Q 390.

the Secretary-General to give regular reports, at least annually, to the Security Council on human rights violation.

ENFORCEMENT

Sanctions

120. When diplomatic efforts at persuading states to comply with the UN's demands have failed, Chapter VII of the Charter prescribes the use of economic methods: embargoes and sanctions (article 41). Although only mentioned briefly in *An Agenda for Peace*,[1] the use of sanctions by the UN, and their effectiveness in securing compliance with its decisions, has been highlighted by the experience of sanctions in Iraq before and after the Gulf War and in Serbia and Montenegro. Witnesses generally agreed that sanctions could be an important part of the UN's armoury in maintaining international peace and security but some thought there were many problems in making them work effectively.

121. Arms embargoes are a sanction under Chapter VII of the Charter used by the Security Council to help reduce the level of conflict and provide an early indication of international dis-approval and could be used where there are serious abuses of human rights. An arms embargo was imposed against South Africa in 1977—the only use of sanctions by the Security Council against a Member State during the Cold War[2] although sanctions were also imposed against Southern Rhodesia in 1966. There are currently arms embargoes in place in respect of Libya, Somalia, Rwanda and parts of former Yugoslavia, for instance. They are not always successful. For example, although there has been a ban on the import of arms into Somalia since January 1992, the country was already awash with arms anyway (it was estimated that there were one million armed men in the country in 1992).[3] Lord Owen pointed out that Yugoslavia was sub-stantially armed already from its own munitions factories.[4] Mr Hogg told the House that, despite the arms embargo, attempts had been made to bring arms into the area from as far afield as Iran.[5] Arms embargoes should not be expected to have dramatic effects on the ground in all situations, although they can act as a useful early warning of the Security Council's inten-tions. The arms embargo against South Africa is held by some to have been a useful persuasive instrument against the South African government.

122. The UN's response to the invasion of Kuwait by Iraq also involved the use of economic sanctions. Iraq was heavily dependent on the export of a single product, oil, and could rela-tively easily be geographically isolated.[6] In the event, military action was also taken against Iraq. After the Gulf War, Security Council Resolution 687 called upon Iraq to fulfil a wide range of undertakings, including the destruction of chemical and biological weapons and nuclear-weapons-usable material and compensation of individuals and corporations affected by the invasion. The principal pressure on Iraq to fulfil these obligations is the sanctions regime which has recently been renewed.[7]

123. Former Yugoslavia provides another prominent case of the UN applying sanctions under Chapter VII, and seeking to enforce them. Initially an arms embargo was applied to the whole region; this now only applies to Serbia, Montenegro and Bosnia-Herzegovina. Security Council Resolution 757 (30 May 1992) imposed trade and economic sanctions on Serbia and Montenegro; SCR 760 (18 June 1992) exempted medical and humanitarian goods from this regime; and SCR 787 (16 November 1992) prohibited the transhipment of strategic and sensi-tive goods along the Danube through Serbia and Montenegro.[8] The sanctions regime allowed goods to be transported through Serbia and Montenegro if it could be proved that they were destined for a third country. The licensing system put in place to implement this had not been fully successful and trans-shipment had proved to be a significant loophole in the regime.[9]

---

[1] Para 41; see also Ev.p 255.
[2] Ev.p 316.
[3] Q 92.
[4] Q 178.
[5] Official Report, 10 February 1993 c. 685W.
[6] Q 371.
[7] See QQ 138–39; Official Report 2 April 1993 c 744.
[8] Official Report, European Standing Committee B, 17 March 1993 c 1; Q 152.
[9] Official Report, European Standing Committee B, 17 March 1993 cc 2–5.

124. Most recently, SCR 820 has put in place a tougher range of measures designed *inter alia* to force the Bosnian Serb leadership to sign the international peace plan and cease military attacks by 26 April 1993. It includes the prohibition of the transport of commodities and products across the land borders or to and from the ports of Serbia-Montenegro; prohibition of all commercial maritime traffic from entering the territorial sea of Serbia-Montenegro; prohibition of the provision of financial and non-financial services to any person or business in Serbia-Montenegro; and impounding of any vehicles, rolling stock, ships or aircraft found to have been used for breaking sanctions. The Foreign Secretary hinted at some of these measures in January when he mentioned the possibility of intensifying sanctions to include the closing of all rail and road frontier crossings.[1] The Foreign Secretary told the House that SCR 820 (which was based on a package prepared by the EC two months earlier at the instigation of the British Government) would turn the sanctions regime into a "blockade" of Serbia-Montenegro.[2] While specifically acting under Chapter VII of the Charter, the Security Council Resolution only authorises states to use "such measures commensurate with the specific circumstances as may be necessary" to enforce this and other relevant resolutions, rather than "all means necessary". (Identical wording was used in SCR 665 in 1990, authorising naval vessels to use force if necessary to stop and search ships attempting to evade sanctions against Iraq. The wording was used to avoid a veto from China or the USSR.)

125. There are two innovative aspects to the sanctions regime in place against parts of the former Yugoslavia. A sanctions coordinator was appointed to keep up the pressure on neighbouring countries and to advise them on how to enforce the sanctions, and the EC has established a number of Sanctions Assistance Missions (SAMs) which are now operating in Bulgaria, Croatia, Hungary and Macedonia. These comprise small teams of customs officials from EC countries (including the UK),[3] whose task is to assist those states in implementing the sanctions regime.[4] In Macedonia in February 1993 members of the Committee met representatives of the SAMs and were impressed by their professionalism in monitoring the transit of goods and any breaches of the sanctions regime. However, they made it clear that they had no power to stop breaches of the sanctions regime, of which the most flagrant was the passage of barges carrying oil from Romania up the Danube into Serbia. Subsequent strengthening of the sanctions regime may now have halted such infringements. FCO officials told us that the procedure by which the SAMs uncovered evidence of collusion in sanctions-breaking by states could be a useful "focus of embarrassment", helping to keep up the pressure to make sanctions more effective.[5] **The EC's sanctions assistance missions in countries neighbouring the former Yugoslavia are a valuable innovation, and we support the Government's commitment of staff to them.**

126. WEU and NATO vessels patrol the Adriatic coast to enforce the blockade on oil deliveries. Lord Owen was critical of some of the early efforts made by the WEU and NATO to enforce the sanctions regime. There had been insufficient efforts made to stop and search tankers in the Adriatic, for instance. He implied this was due to a lack of political will by the WEU governments concerned.[6] Mr Hogg told the House in April that since November 1992 the combined NATO/WEU operation had challenged 9,000 vessels, boarded 599 and diverted 137. This had been a "most valuable contribution to efforts to block international trade".[7]

127. Mr Hogg argued that the experience of sanctions-monitoring and enforcement during the Gulf conflict had helped build up a body of expertise which was being applied in the former Yugoslavia, but thought that the SAMs needed to be "further reinforced".[8] The Foreign Secretary believed the sanctions had been effective in their early stages but had then weakened; he was not satisfied with the position in January. Mr Hogg told the House that five barges had breached sanctions by delivering oil to Serbia via the Danube, and another six oil deliveries by barges to Montenegro via the Adriatic.[9] The passing of SCR 820 (see paragraph 124 above) may lead to a much stricter enforcement of the sanctions, possibly including the use of military

[1] Q 277.
[2] Official Report, 19 April 1993 c 21.
[3] Official Report, 14 April 1993, c 827.
[4] Q 515.
[5] Q 515.
[6] Q 178.
[7] Official Report, 23 April 1993 c 244W.
[8] Q 152.
[9] Official Report, 10 February 1993 c. 685W.

force. The UK Government has also provided £100,000 towards the establishment of a communications network along the Danube to improve the effectiveness of the sanctions regime.[1]

128. Some witnesses were disparaging about the effectiveness of sanctions. Professor Roberts listed five fundamental problems of economic sanctions: they may be ineffective due to sanctions evasions; they may have no effect on the policy of the target states even if effective; they can affect the innocent in the target state before the guilty; they make the inhabitants more rather than less dependent on their government; and the transition from sanctions to military action is liable to be intensely controversial. He believed they were a "blunt, unreliable and controversial instrument".[2] It is certainly true that their historical record has been mixed, though the combination of a mandatory UN arms embargo and EC and other sanctions against South Africa had a telling effect, over a period of time, on the policies of the government of South Africa.

129. Even if fully enforced, sanctions can fail to have the intended effect of pressuring governments to change policy, but may be all too effective in penalising the population of the affected state. As our predecessor Committee concluded in respect of Iraq, "the burden of sanctions ... will bear most heavily on the Iraqi people as a whole".[3] To alleviate this, the Security Council exempted the import of medical materials from sanctions and allowed the Iraqi government to sell oil up to the value of $1.6bn so long as the proceeds went towards compensating affected nationals and corporations affected and for the import of food and medical supplies. Mr Hogg told us that the Iraqi government had refused to sell the oil, so the money was not yet available.[4] Import of medical materials is also exempted from sanctions against Serbia and Montenegro.

130. Professor Roberts argued that more creative thought was needed on measures that could be taken to enforce the UN's authority short of military force.[5] The United Nations Association argued that sanctions could be made more effective by the stationing of UN customs officers at customs posts on the relevant borders[6]—perhaps on the same lines as the customs officers from Member States participating in the EC Sanctions Assistance Missions in former Yugoslavia. Dr Taylor, while suggesting that a relatively unsupervised sanctions regime might be used as a first step in bringing a state into line, argued that the eventual use of military force to enforce sanctions should be considered.[7] One step that the UN could take without further ado would be to agree in principle that sanctions regimes, when imposed, should amount to a blockade from the start. It is clear from the experience in former Yugoslavia that the sanctions regime did not bite for a considerable time; while sanctions certainly had the desired result of damaging the economy of Serbia,[8] this took some time; and the other intention—that of forcing the Serbian government to ensure compliance with the Vance-Owen plan has not been realised. **Limited sanctions do not seem to us to have proved successful; if the UN wishes to use sanctions as an effective weapon they need to be accompanied from the start by a blockade, by land, sea and air, and by a sophisticated range of controls over commercial, financial and trading mechanisms.** To enhance credibility, the UN needs to establish a system by which action can be taken against violators who breach mandatory sanctions. A precedent was set in the case of South Africa whereby the UN Anti-Apartheid Committee published lists of violators. Due to state jurisdiction laws, the UN itself would have difficulty taking effective action against offenders but the governments of individual countries concerned would thereby be pressurised to prosecute when appropriate.

131. Sir Crispin Tickell and Professor Alan James argued that sanctions caused problems for some states whose trade diminished markedly as a result of applying them.[9] During the Gulf War, Jordan, Egypt and Syria were particularly affected;[10] in the case of former Yugoslavia, states such as Hungary, Macedonia and Romania are suffering. The UN Charter attempts to solve this problem by giving such states the right "to consult the Security Council with regard

---

[1] Official Report, 14 April 1993 c 827.
[2] Ev. p 310.
[3] HC(1990-91) 143-I, para 3.10.
[4] Q 138, and Official Report, 2 April 1993 c 744; Q 339.
[5] Ev.p 310.
[6] Ev.p 269–270.
[7] Q 408.
[8] Eg. Q 123.
[9] QQ 371,408.
[10] QQ 339,371.

to a solution of those [economic] problems" (article 50). This does not provide a means for compensating affected states, and the Secretary-General recommends in *Agenda for Peace* that Security Council members develop a mechanism for ensuring that financial help is made available in these circumstances. The United Nations Association also stressed the need for more resources to be directed towards third countries affected by the imposition of sanctions.[1] **While sanctions can never be 100% effective they could be made more effective than they have proved in the past. In general they are effective only if maintained over a long period;[2] so the international community, if it wishes to encourage states to participate fully in implementing them, may have to be prepared, in effect, to pay them to do so. We recommend that the government encourage discussion within the Security Council to develop a mechanism for providing financial help to states affected by sanctions. If Member States are committed to using third countries as a significant tool of enforcement, they will have to be prepared both for the cost they will incur in terms of loss of trade, and to back them up with force if necessary.**

Military enforcement

132. Armed force is the apex of interventionism: while a robust sanctions regime against a country is a significant show of coercion, air, sea or ground attacks on it are a far more dramatic indication of international condemnation and are likely to be rare. The point at which it is decided that sanctions will not achieve the desired end and military force must be employed is inevitably determined by political factors. For instance, Sir Brian Urquhart argued in the context of military action against **Iraq** that "no determination about the adequacy of sanctions was ever made by the [Security] Council". Others argued that by passing resolution 678 the Council implicitly recognised their inadequacy.[3] Whatever the merits of this particular case, it is clear that any decision to move from economic to military means of enforcement will **always** be controversial, as there appears to be no objective method of determining at what point sanctions become effective.

133. The coalition operation against Iraq in 1991 provides the most clear-cut case of military enforcement in respect of a breach of the Charter. Our predecessor committee regarded this action as a landmark in the history of the Organisation.[4] In **Somalia**, large-scale military force was employed to ensure that the decisions of the Security Council respecting a ceasefire and the unimpeded distribution of humanitarian aid were respected. Security Council Resolution 794 specifically noted the application of Chapter VII of the Charter and authorised the US-led forces to use "all necessary means" to fulfil their mandate. The decision implicitly conceded that previous measures—diplomatic pressure, an arms embargo, unarmed observers to monitor the ceasefire, and the stationing of 500 UN soldiers with a traditional peace-keeping mandate,—had failed to achieve the UN's aims. The fact that the UN-authorised force, UNITAF, has been replaced by a UN force (UNOSOM II) with an equally robust mandate in terms of rules of engagement, powers to disarm, etc—is an indication in this case that the UN is prepared to enforce its decisions more vigorously than was previously the case.

134. While members of the Committee were in Somalia, it was impressed on them by the soldiers that they met that they were much happier working under their more robust rules of engagement than they would have been under the mandate apparently in force in Bosnia. One commander told us that he believed that many of the countries who had contributed troops to operation Restore Hope, and who intended to contribute to UNOSOM II, would not have done so if it were not carried out under a Chapter VII mandate. It seemed clear that, given the chaotic circumstances prevailing in parts of Somalia, only a force both more heavily armed than conventional UN peacekeepers, and with rules of engagement that allowed them to use arms aggressively where necessary, could achieve the aims of the UN. If the consent of each clan, sub-clan or local armed gang were needed before convoys of food could be moved, the UN would not be able to do the job required of it. Equally, the parts of the mandate requiring cantonment of arms, re-establishment of communications, basic health and education infrastructure and the rebuilding of the demolished towns and cities only seemed to be possible with the active support of the military machine. The Security Council has now strengthened further the mandate of UNOSOM II to authorise it to take all necessary measures against those

---

[1] Ev.p 269.
[2] See eg Q 371.
[3] Ev.p 270.
[4] Third Report, Session 1990-91 (HC(90–91)143) para 2.3.

responsible for attacks on UN soldiers on 5 June 1993,[1] and retaliatory action began on 11 and 12 June 1993.

135. Somalia is obviously a very special case; starvation was widespread, most semblances of a national authority had vanished as a result of the terrible civil war and the organs of the state with which the UN is accustomed to deal had disintegrated. The UN's efforts at rebuilding the country will have to start from the basis that traditional, state-based power structures simply do not exist. However, **it is probable that many of the future disasters of the world will be located in similar situations to that found in Somalia, where civil war, territorial disputes and a disparity between geographic boundaries and ethnic realities may mean that the UN may not be able to negotiate with governments. Equally, it is in just such circumstances that the demand for the UN's help may be most pressing, and where the use of military force to ensure the UN's help is delivered may be needed most and where there may be the greatest unease about the employment of such force. We believe that the amount of force used should be such as not to alienate substantial proportions of a population. Inordinate force can be wholly counterproductive and endanger the activities of NGOs.**

136. As indicated in paragraph 68 above, in the former **Yugoslavia**, UNPROFOR's original mandate was a peace-keeping one, not a peace-enforcement one. Peace-keeping in Croatia and the military assistance to humanitarian operations throughout the region, including the protection of convoys of aid and movement of refugees did not fall into the category of enforcement operations. As discussed above, however, there have been a series of additions to UNPROFOR's mandate, to enforce the air exclusion zone[2] and economic sanctions, to allow troops in Croatia to use military force if their movement was interfered with and, more recently, to protect safe havens and begin to implement the peace-plan drawn up by Mr Cyrus Vance and Lord Owen, co-chairmen of the conference convened jointly by the European Community and the United Nations to try to resolve the conflict in Bosnia.[3]

137. The principle of an air exclusion zone, banning military flights, was authorised by the Security Council in October 1992 but the resolution did not specify the means by which it might be enforced. The air exclusion zone is monitored by UN observers in airfields throughout the former Yugoslavia.[4] Members of the Committee visited a team of UN Military Observers at Pristina military airfield in Kosovo and were impressed by the professional and extremely thorough way in which they were detailing every movement of aircraft in and out of the base. Mr Hogg told us in December that, while there had been many infringements of the exclusion zone, there had been no combat operations; the Security Council had to decide whether to pass a resolution preemptively authorising military enforcement of the exclusion zone, or to wait until a breach occurred and then do so.[5] Lord Owen told us on 10 December that the no-fly zone could be maintained by negotiation, without the use of force; but that, if eventually a Chapter VII determination was reached, enforcement would be needed.[6] However, "you do not threaten what you are not prepared to commit": following a decision to enforce the zone, action would have to be taken to ensure those on the ground took the UN seriously.[7] In the event, the Security Council held back from passing the necessary resolution until April 1993, perhaps influenced by the argument that enforcement during the winter could have jeopardised the UN's humanitarian effort on the ground in Croatia and Bosnia.[8] Although UN-authorised, the operation to enforce the air exclusion zone is NATO-run.[9]

138. Military force has been authorised to enforce and tighten the sanctions regime in place in parts of former Yugoslavia. NATO and WEU naval contingents have been monitoring shipping in the Adriatic and on the Danube for possible breaches in the regime, but did not have the power forcibly to turn back or disable vessels breaking sanctions until the passing of SCR 820 in April 1993.

---

[1] SCR 837 (1993).
[2] SCR 816.
[3] SCR 836.
[4] Q 113.
[5] QQ 113–114.
[6] Q 172.
[7] *Ibid.*
[8] Q 172.
[9] Official Report, 1 April 1993 c 499.

139. During the Committee's visit to Geneva and in formal and informal meetings with Lord Owen, the Committee has had the opportunity to discuss the plan he and Mr Vance drew up for a long term solution to the conflict in Bosnia. The Vance-Owen plan includes a map redrawing the internal administrative borders in Bosnia. If the plan were implemented, Bosnia would be divided into ten largely autonomous provinces, with relatively little power vested in central government. Besides the map, the plan sets out detailed constitutional provisions and arrangements for military disengagement. A corollary of its implementation would be the withdrawal of the troops of each of the three factions from parts of the territories they control, including territory seized during the fighting.[1]

140. After the plan was drawn up in January 1993, the EC and the UN endeavoured both to persuade all parties in Bosnia, Croatia and Serbia to accept it and to agree how the international community might guarantee it. There has been a debate between the major powers about possible use of military force to ensure compliance with the Vance-Owen plan. Options considered have included selective air strikes to cut off supply routes from Serbia into Bosnian Serb-held areas in eastern Bosnia. Such air strikes could be regarded as an extreme form of ensuring compliance with the arms embargo and the blockade. Other options considered have ranged from siting UN personnel on the Serb-Bosnian border to large scale intervention by armed forces on the ground, using troops from NATO countries and from some non-NATO countries, including Russia. On 24 May 1993 the governments of the USA, Russia, the UK, France and Spain agreed a "Joint action programme on Bosnia" which included an endorsement of the idea of "Safe Areas" within which UN troops might protect threatened Muslim minorities in Bosnia and backed the "Vance-Owen *process*". The five signatories stated they were firmly united and firmly committed to taking the steps set out in this programme and would work closely with the UN and involved regional organisations.[2] This agreement was followed on 4 June 1993 by Security Council resolution 836 giving UNPROFOR enforcement powers under Chapter VII of the Charter, *inter alia*, to protect safe areas in Bosnia. The Resolution also "affirms that these safe areas are a temporary measure and that the primary objective remains to reverse the consequences of the use of force and to allow all persons displaced from their homes in the Republic of Bosnia and Herzegovina to return to their homes in peace, beginning *inter alia* with the prompt implementation of the Vance-Owen plan in areas where these have been agreed by the parties directly concerned".

141. The Vance-Owen plan represented in practice an attempt by the international community to impose a new administrative and constitutional structure on Bosnia, as well as arrangements for military disengagement. It differed from, for example, the Paris Agreement on Cambodia, which set out interim transitional arrangements until UN-run elections produced a constituent assembly. It could also have required an open-ended commitment by the UN to provide anything up to 30,000 troops to police the planned territorial arrangements. Lord Owen and the EC have now acknowledged that the original Vance-Owen plan is now dead following bilateral agreements made between Serbs and Croats in Bosnia. **Disagreement between the USA and European powers about whether, and how, to enforce compliance with the Vance-Owen plan for Bosnia has illustrated, at the least, the difficulties of UN-sponsored efforts to impose a settlement and enforce peace from outside.**

142. In **Iraq**, aircraft of the coalition forces have enforced an air-exclusion zone in pursuance of SCR 688. Aircraft violating the zone have been shot down (13 and 18 January 1993), aircraft of the coalition have attacked Iraqi air defence facilities and command and control facilities. On 17 January, American cruise missiles were used with the declared objective of attacking a facility connected with the Iraqi weapons of mass destruction programme.[3] The action against the weapons facility was stated by the Secretary-General to be within the mandate of SCR 687,[4] but its legitimacy has been questioned. The question of how far enforcement of the air exclusion zone was legitimised by the Security Council has been equally controversial. It is argued that such action was taken in pursuance of SCR 688, but that resolution has taken the UN into disputed territory.

143. In this section we have concentrated on the political and strategic considerations affecting the use of military force to enforce Security Council decisions. But, as in other UN's

---

[1] Agreement for Peace in Bosnia and Herzegovina, International Conference on the former Yugoslavia, 2 January 1993.
[2] The Washington Agreement, Joint action programme on Bosnia, 24 May 1993.
[3] Official Report, 13 January 1993 cc 1012–13 and 18 January 1993 c 23; Q 304.
[4] Official Report 18 January 1993 c 24.

endeavours, there remains a key point about mobilising forces. Putting aside questions of the *form* military intervention takes, and the structure of command and control, will Member States be prepared to commit troops (and the resources to support them) anyway? The Secretary-General states: "Member States are keen to participate in peace-keeping operations. Military observers and infantry are invariably available in the required numbers".[1] This may be optimistic, given the reported difficulties faced by the Secretary-General in finding forces for operations in Rwanda, Mozambique and Cyprus and uncertainty about states' willingness to contribute further forces to Bosnia. It is possible that there would be even greater difficulties in finding troops to serve in UN operations, including peace enforcement operations, which laid them open to much greater risk of attack. On the other hand, our conversations with soldiers in the Unified Task Force (UNITAF) operation in Somalia revealed a greater willingness to participate in operations which, while perhaps riskier than traditional peace-keeping, permitted the UN forces a more robust response in defending themselves and fulfilling their objectives.

144. It will presumably be easier for the Secretary-General to find troops, and for the Security Council to authorise enforcement actions, if contributing Member States are confident that the UN has the capacity to use them effectively. Ways in which UN military operations could be structured in future are discussed in the section on institutional change below (paragraphs 224–244).

145. The more frequent use of military force under Chapter VII could pose a threat to Security Council unanimity. States may be opposed to military intervention without consent on principle, or because their own interests in an area ultimately outweigh their commitment to international agreements. Russia managed to delay consideration of stronger economic measures against Serbia and Montenegro for some time and still remains ambivalent about military options. China has regularly abstained on such issues, notably on the enforcement of the Bosnian air-exclusion zone. **Mandates for the military enforcement of UN actions should be as clear as the consensus-based nature of UN politics allows. Enforcement action by the UN will only make practical sense if the Member States are willing to provide the military and logistical resources required and if the political will to use those resources exists, recognising that a process of enforcement may take a great many years and lead to large numbers of casualties.**

COOPERATION WITH REGIONAL ARRANGEMENTS

146. Under Chapter VIII of the UN Charter, the Security Council shall "encourage the development of pacific settlement of local disputes" through regional arrangements, and Member States shall "make every effort to achieve pacific settlement of local disputes" through regional arrangements before referring them to the Security Council. This relationship is stressed in the North Atlantic Treaty, under which NATO Member States are bound to respect the UN Charter and the primary responsibility of the Security Council. The Secretary-General notes that during the Cold War the value of regional organisations in settling disputes was impaired and indeed their existence sometimes militated against the proper working of the Charter.[2] Now, however, the Secretary-General believes that regional arrangements could "contribute to a deeper sense of participation, consensus and democratization in international affairs".[3] His declared aim is a new division of labour, in which the UN will retain its primacy in the maintenance of international peace and security, while its burden is lightened by the active involvement of appropriate regional arrangements and agencies.[4]

147. The Charter is unspecific about the nature of the "regional arrangements" covered by Chapter VIII, but in practice they have included treaty-based organisations such as the Organisation of African Unity (OAU), the Organisation of American States (OAS), the Economic Community of West African States (ECOWAS) and in the former Yugoslavia, the EC, CSCE and NATO. Sometimes they have worked alone, with the approval of the UN, sometimes in cooperation with UN efforts. Their tasks have included mediation in conflicts (OAU in Sudan, EC and UN in former Yugoslavia), cease-fire monitoring (OAU in Rwanda, EC in Croatia), peace-keeping (ECOWAS in Liberia), delivery of UN humanitarian relief (EC in former Yugoslavia), monitoring of sanctions (CSCE, WEU and NATO in former

---

[1] *An Agenda for Peace*, para 51.
[2] *Ibid*, para 60.
[3] *Ibid* para 64.
[4] Report on the Work of the Organisation, para 115.

Yugoslavia), human rights monitoring (UN and OAS in Haiti, CSCE in former Yugoslavia) and election-monitoring (OAS and UN in Nicaragua, OAU and UN in Mozambique).

148. Sir John Thomson was "apprehensive" about the emphasis the Secretary-General put on regional organisations, although he understood the temptation to shift some of the burdens facing the UN.[1] Witnesses were cautious and frequently sceptical as to the extent to which regional arrangements could fulfil the expectations the Secretary-General placed in them. It is not always possible to get them to take on difficult tasks. In the past, the UN has sometimes encouraged the handling of a crisis by the relevant regional organisation, only to find that important aspects of the problem remain on its shoulders.[2] The Foreign Secretary had hoped the Gulf Cooperation Council (GCC) would have taken more decisive steps to develop collective security in the Gulf region, but little had been achieved.[3] There is no single powerful regional organisation in some parts of the world, notably South-East Asia, and where there is one it may not be properly equipped to handle crises (for example the OAU in Chad in 1981[4]).

149. The United Nations Association points out that most conflicts occur within and between developing countries, so most demand for regional forces will fall on the areas which can least afford them.[5] Sometimes deference to regionalism has delayed the resolution of questions in accordance with UN principles—Professor Higgins cited the case of Western Sahara.[6] Dr Gwyn Prins of the University of Cambridge believed that the challenge for the international community is to "clarify rapidly relations between regional and global institutions".[7]

150. There can be problems when several regional arrangements co-exist in one area. The crisis in **former Yugoslavia** represented perhaps the best opportunity to date for regional arrangements to take on work which might otherwise have been done by the UN. Witnesses were not impressed by the work of regional organisations in the area. Dr Prins described it as a "monumental failure of EC foreign policy ... a prolonged failure of regional response". The failure of the EC and other European regional institution led to an enlarging UN rôle whose rationale was partly to "paper over European deficiencies".[8] Some in the EC saw the Yugoslav crisis as a means to advance the case for a Common Foreign and Security policy vis à vis its potential rivalry with NATO. Sir Anthony Parsons stated that the EC, as the appropriate regional organisation, made a series of diplomatic errors and failed to take any preventive action *before* the conflict started. Once the UN was involved, there was inadequate cooperation between the two.[9] Lord Owen pointed out that, at the start, the United States did not want to be involved in Yugoslavia and the EC was "not too keen" to involve the UN.[10] The United Nations Association believed that the CSCE was "totally ill-equipped" to tackle the Yugoslav crisis.[11]

151. The Secretary of State for Defence noted that the "theological dispute" between NATO and WEU over whose task it was to provide a naval presence in the Adriatic was "not an edifying experience"; the resulting duplication was "an inadequate and unfortunate use of scarce resources".[12] The FCO argued that the original division between peacemaking by the EC and peace-keeping by the UN was "not a very helpful distinction", but that lessons had been learned and the efforts of the two organisations had been fused, with the London conference being the first ever formalized approach between the UN and a regional organisation.[13] As a result of this new approach the two organisation were working together "remarkably well" and there was no conflict between them.[14] The Foreign Secretary told us that the WEU-NATO

[1] Q 382.
[2] See Ev.p 313,179,273.
[3] Q 306.
[4] Ev.p 273.
[5] Ev.p 273.
[6] Ev.p 179.
[7] Ev.p 251.
[8] Ev.p 249.
[9] *International Relations*, December 1992 p 198.
[10] Q 185.
[11] Ev.p 273.
[12] Speech to RUSI, 20 January 1993; also Official Report, 9 March 1993 c 778.
[13] Q 40, Ev.p 2.
[14] Q 46.

cooperation was now working more effectively[1] and described the EC-UN framework as "elaborate and energetic".[2] Unless care is taken to demarcate exactly who should do what, arrangements may become more elaborate at the expense of their energy. Baroness Chalker pointed out that effective cooperation between the UN and regional organisations was also needed in the humanitarian context. She told us that the involvement of the EC humanitarian office (ECHO) in former Yugoslavia had not started well. There had been too great an insistence by the EC in trying to set up a parallel organisation to UNHCR as a way of achieving greater visibility for the EC; had this approach been pursued there would have been a waste of resources. The British Red Cross also told us that there had been problems with coordination by the EC, though their working relationship was generally good.[3] The EC had now set up a Task Force to ensure that the EC effort worked with the UN rather than as a rival to it, although some tensions remained.[4]

152. **NATO** has played a key rôle in the Yugoslav crisis. It has agreed to undertake peace-keeping operations under the auspices of the CSCE and has contributed a mobile headquarters to UNPROFOR, a NATO naval squadron to the Adriatic in support of Security Council Resolutions and fighter aircraft to deter attacks on UN troops protecting safe areas and to enforce the no-fly zone.[5] The contribution which NATO and its Member States can make to the military operations of the UN in future is discussed in paras 238–240 below; as far as its rôle as a regional organisation is concerned, there is unlikely to be any decrease in the range of problems the UN will be faced with and NATO will continue to be in demand for many of them. The Foreign Secretary told us that although the Adriatic operation, for instance, was "not ideal" it was coordinated well enough for there to be no operational problems. NATO was now fulfilling its commitment to make assets available for UN operations and he saw NATO as being increasingly useful in this kind of operation.[6] Lord Owen told us that the UN operation in former Yugoslavia had benefited greatly from the NATO involvement, but stressed that the command of the operation had come from a UN headquarters rather than an NATO headquarters.[7] The Secretary-General of NATO argued that the Alliance was "a natural partner for the UN" in European security affairs[8] and that cooperation between NATO and the UN in handling regional instabilities was a perfectly viable model, though he believed that leadership of such operations should remain with the United Nations.[9]

153. Regional organisations can also be seen as biased by the parties concerned.[10] Lord Owen warned that there were dangers for the UN in a regional organisation becoming involved because the organisation would be "committed" in the area. The choice of the troops in a combined UN-regional force must remain under the control of the Secretary-General to avoid any accusations of undue influence by regional powers.[11]

154. In **Liberia**, where a civil war has continued for four years following the death of former leader Samuel Doe, the task of peace-keeping has been left to ECOMOG (the ECOWAS Monitoring and Observing Group), a peace-keeping force organised by the Economic Community of West African States (ECOWAS). Liberia appears to be one crisis in which the Secretary-General has achieved the goal of a regional organisation keeping the burden of a substantial peace-keeping operation (ECOMOG is 15,000 strong) away from the UN. But at what cost? There is no agreement among the parties that the peace-keeping force is acting impartially and there is no sign that an end to the conflict, or the planned free elections,[12] are any nearer.

155. In his evidence, Professor Roberts cited three ways in which the UN is better equipped to deal with international problems than regional organizations: it has wide powers, laid down in the Charter; it has, in the Security Council, a mechanism for reaching tough and often con-

[1] QQ 284–85.
[2] Q 53, 12 October 1992.
[3] Q 251.
[4] QQ 345–47.
[5] HC 205–vi, Ev.p 115.
[6] Q 285.
[7] Q 186.
[8] Speech to the Munich Conference for Security Policy, 7 February 1993.
[9] Speech at the Academy for Peace and International Security, Monaco, 5 March 1993.
[10] See eg. Ev.p 299.
[11] Q 185.
[12] Secretary-General's Annual Report, 1992, para 120.

troversial decisions quickly; and it has an unrivalled reputation for impartial good offices and peace-keeping.[1]

156. Undoubtedly, there is a case for saying that some involvement of the UN in peace-keeping and conflict resolution is always a good thing, because of its impartiality, universality and expertise. However, given the pressures under which it is working, Member States cannot expect the Organisation to become operationally active in settling all the disputes brought to it, and more joint operations between the UN and appropriate regional organisations seem probable. **We endorse the shift in attitude shown in** *An Agenda for Peace* **and the acceptance that there has to be a partnership between regional organisations and the UN, not a shuffling off of responsibilities between them.**[2]

157. It is not always possible for regional organisations to undertake to solve, let alone actually solve, conflicts and other crises. There may not be any existing organisation, and if one does exist it may not be appropriately resourced. Where there is one, Member States should follow the spirit of the Charter by attempting to solve local disputes through regional arrangements, either alone or in conjunction with the UN.[3] **All recommendations for the improvement of the UN's performance must start from the basis that it neither can nor should try to do everything. Its job should be as much to help others to solve problems as to solve them itself. Hence our emphasis on the need for the UN wherever possible to take advantage of the expertise and experience of other players, be they NATO, NGOs or others. But the** *authority* **of the United Nations in matters of international security is crucial: we agree with witnesses[4] that force should not be employed by regional organisations on behalf of the UN without the explicit authority of the Security Council.**

VI FINANCING THE UNITED NATIONS

158. In *An Agenda for Peace*, the Secretary-General describes a "chasm" which has developed between the tasks entrusted to the UN and the financial means provided to it.[5] The financial position of the UN has long been precarious, but the recent explosion of demands on the Organisation have greatly increased the crisis. The number of disputes in which the UN is now expected to be asked to intervene has substantially increased and is likely to continue to increase. This leads to resource demands which the UN currently has difficulty in meeting.[6] In 1978 the total arrears owing to the UN were assessed by the FCO at $120.3 million, a situation which they commented could not continue indefinitely.[7] At 31 October 1992 the total arrears owed to the Organisation amounted to $1.25 billion[8]; the money spent by the UN on peace-keeping in 1992 was approximately $1.4 billion.[9]

159. There are two aspects to the current crisis in funding the UN. One is **the overall position of the UN's finances**, and the second is **paying for the UN's peace endeavours.** The situation has been exacerbated by the growing demands placed on the UN and the expectations placed in it, while at the same time, Member States do not seem any more willing than before to pay their contributions. For instance, there have been recent reports of the Secretary-General having to withdraw UN guards from Northern Iraq due to lack of funds, and the recent Russian veto over the future financing arrangements for the UNFYCIP operation in Cyprus for a short time cast doubt on the Organisation's ability to continue financing it. Both these operations have been paid for by voluntary contributions by Member States: if the resources are not forthcoming, UN personnel will have to be withdrawn. The UN operation in Cyprus has for a very long time depended on the forbearance of troop-contributing states. At a time when the UN is being looked to by some for the virtual administration of countries, which would be a massively expensive undertaking (e.g. the $2 billion cost of UNTAC in Cambodia and the proposed $1.5 billion cost of UNOSOM II in Somalia), these are not encouraging precedents. One witness

---

[1] Ev.p 314.
[2] See Ev.p 313.
[3] cf Q 382.
[4] eg. Professor Higgins, Ev.p 179; cf also the Secretary of State for Defence, speech to the Royal United Services Institute, 20 January 1993.
[5] *An Agenda for Peace*, para 69.
[6] Ev.p 242, Q52.
[7] *British Policy towards the United Nations*, Foreign Policy Documents No.28, 1978, p 34.
[8] Ev.p 63.
[9] *Financing an Effective United Nations*, Report of the Independent Advisory Group on Financing, April 1993 p 14.

argued that it was no longer a question of whether the system would break down, but when.[1] Sir Crispin Tickell pointed out that Secretaries General have always had to spend too much of their time looking for money at the expense of their main tasks.[2]

160. The amounts of money involved in running the UN itself are not very great in global terms. Sir Anthony Parsons notes that the budget of the UN Headquarters in New York is roughly the same as that of the British Foreign and Commonwealth Office.[3] The combined cost of the UN regular and peace-keeping budgets for 1992 is estimated to be less than the cost of two Stealth bombers or running the New York police and fire departments for one year.[4] In the last few years (partly at the behest of the UK) the real terms budget of the Organisation has not increased.[5] However, expenditure on peace-keeping has increased greatly.

How the UN is financed

161. The financing of the UN is extremely complex. The UN and the organisations of the UN system are financed by a system of assessed and voluntary contributions from Member States. Assessed contributions, which cover the UN regular budget and peace-keeping activities, are mandatory and their payment legally binding on Member States. Voluntary contributions are paid towards the cost of UN activities in humanitarian and development assistance. The UN regular budget is set biennially and is financed by contributions from Member States; the capacity of each state to pay, and therefore its assessment is calculated according to its average national income over a ten year base period. The UK assessment, for instance, is 5.02% of the regular budget (the fifth highest payment), while that for the US is 25% and Albania's is 0.01%. The peace-keeping budget is normally financed on an ad hoc special scale for each operation: developing countries pay one fifth or one-tenth of their regular rate while the five permanent members pay a compensating surcharge; in 1992 the UK paid 6.102%, the US 30.87% and Albania 0.002%.[6] Currently the UN is operating a policy of zero real growth under which new activities mandated by the General Assembly have to be financed either from a small contingency fund, by redeployment of existing resources or by deferment to the next budgetary round.[7] Most of the humanitarian and development activities of the UN are financed by voluntary contributions.

The current crisis

162. Sir David Hannay told us that "It is the arrears that are the real problem",[8] a point of view shared by all witnesses. Dr Prins noted that at the end of 1991, Member States owed the UN more than $816 million: $439 on the regular budget and $377 million on peace-keeping.[9] At the end of 1992, Member States owed the organisation $500 million, mostly in unpaid dues from previous years.[10] The payment record of the United States was singled out for criticism by several witnesses,[11] one of whom described their position as being "inexcusable".[12] The Foreign Secretary told us that the US could not "reconcile its position in the world today with the existence of these debts".[13] For some years the US has withheld payments to the UN on political grounds, for instance when Congress or the US administration disapproved either of specific policies or programmes or the general stance of the Organisation. A powerful anti-UN movement in Congress ensured that large sums were withheld; a further reason was a desire to use non-payment of some funds as a lever to encourage greater budgetary transparency in the UN budget. Sir Crispin Tickell expressed the view that for many years the US had failed to pay its subscriptions and indeed had done "all they could to spite the UN".[14] The US share of the total arrears to the UN at the end of 1991 was more than $266 million of the regular bud-

---

[1] Professor Groom, Ev p 245

[2] Q 356.

[3] *International Relations*, December 1992 p 198.

[4] *Financing an Effective United Nations*, Report of the Independent Advisory Group on Financing, April 1993 p 6.

[5] Ev.pp 62–63.

[6] Ev.pp 62, 77–79; The UK share of the cost of peace-keeping operations has been increased in 1993 to 6.373% (HC Deb 17 May 1993, Col 42W).

[7] Ev.p 62.

[8] Q 53.

[9] Ev.p 248–249.

[10] *Financing an Effective United Nations*, p 8.

[11] eg. the United Nations Association, Ev.p 260.

[12] Ev.p 259.

[13] Ev.p 247, Q 65.

[14] Q 384.

get and $141 million on the peace-keeping budget.[1] At their height, the US arrears accounted for 80% of the UN's internal indebtedness. However, since 1990, the US has been paying its dues in full, plus $40 million per annum in payment of arrears, which at the end of 1992 represented less than 50% of the UN's internal indebtedness.[2] FCO witnesses noted that the Bush administration had made "major efforts in the last two years to get back on the right road of paying its assessments".[3]

163. The UK's payment record has always been impeccable. Although, because of the size of its assessment, late payment by the US is the largest single factor in the UN's arrears, there are other non-payers. Russia, for instance, has a payment problem which is according to Sir David Hannay not due to a lack of political will but to a lack of money.[4] Russia's peace-keeping assessment alone for 1992 was $175 million, and the assessed contributions of Russia, Ukraine and Belarus, represent some 11% of the UN's regular budget assessment. In 1992 none of these states paid any peace-keeping contributions and they paid only a small percentage of their regular budget contributions. (Russia intended to pay $130 million of its arrears, primarily to the regular budget, by the end of March 1993.[5]). Other states with a poor payment record include Brazil, which owed $33 million at the end of October 1992 and South Africa which owed $49 million.[6] In some cases payments have been withheld for political reasons, in others because of economic difficulties; in the long term it may be that countries with economic problems will pose more of a problem for the UN than those which have withheld payment for political reasons.

164. Late payment is as much of a problem as non-payment. Although states are supposed to pay within 30 days of assessment, many states are permanently months or years behind, even if they pay up in the end. The only sanction the UN has is that, if a Member State's arrears exceed two years' annual subscription, it forfeits its vote in the General Assembly unless the Assembly is satisfied that failure to pay is for reasons beyond the member's control.[7] This is not enough of a threat. One of the reasons why some countries are often technically in arrears is that their fiscal cycles are out of step with that of the UN. The UN's financial year starts with the calendar year, and assessments are sent out on 1 January. However, the US does not pay its dues until the start of its fiscal year in October, and Japan does not pay until the UN contribution is approved by the Diet in June. Both states (which account for 37.45% of the regular budget between them) are therefore in arrears for several months of the year. Similarly, the UK's financial year starts in April; the problem of arrears is mitigated by paying the contribution to the regular budget in two tranches, one in January and the balance in April.

FUNDING THE REGULAR BUDGET

165. The Secretary-General made a number of suggestions for improving the UN's financial position in *An Agenda for Peace* (summarised in Annex C), and also asked an Independent Advisory Group, chaired by Mr Paul Volcker and Mr Shijuro Ogata, to examine ways of improving the UN's financial situation. We have also received suggestions from witnesses during the inquiry. However, by far the most significant problem facing the UN is non-payment, or late payment, by members. The Advisory Group state bluntly that "if all governments paid their assessment contributions in full and on time there would be no serious UN financial problem".

166. The Secretary-General's proposals include charging interest on outstanding assessed contributions, allowing budgetary surpluses to be retained and authorising the Secretary-General to borrow commercially. In his report he also mentions other suggestions: taxing airline travel; authorization for the UN to borrow from the World Bank and the IMF and encouraging contributions to the UN by corporations and individuals by means of tax exemptions.

---

[1] Ev.p 248.
[2] *Financing an Effective United Nations*, p 8.
[3] Q 53; details of recent US payments, totalling $385.4 million, are at Ev. p 63.
[4] Q 53.
[5] Ev.p 63.
[6] Ev.pp 71, 75.
[7] Charter, Article 19.

167. The Secretary-General's ideas in *An Agenda for Peace* were welcomed by some witnesses, even though one called them "modest" and another, though admitting they were "sensible measures" believed they were not sufficient to solve the problem.[1] FCO witnesses were in favour of retaining the present system of financing rather than creating new methods.[2] The idea of encouraging private donations to the UN, for instance, has been suggested regularly over the years. The Independent Advisory Group argued that private donations might lessen the control the Member States have over the organisation. The point made by the FCO in 1978, that the private sector would be unlikely to want to give funds to pay off the deficits created by Member States withholding payments still probably holds true, as does the conclusion that there would be strong opposition from Member States and commercial interests to any levy on air transport, etc.[3] **We do not believe that donations from the private sector would have much impact on the UN's financial position; furthermore, it would be inappropriate for an organisation of sovereign states to be significantly dependent on private donations.**

168. The Independent Advisory Group concludes that the system of assessed contributions to the regular budget should remain in place. However, it proposes that, instead of a single annual payment being expected of Member States, they should pay their dues in four instalments. States such as the US which normally pay their dues late in the UN's fiscal year should appropriate them earlier; i.e. the US would pay the first quarter of its annual dues at the beginning of the US fiscal year prior to the relevant UN fiscal year. Thus the US would be three month in credit rather than nine months behind. Coupled with this system, the Advisory Group agree with the Secretary-General's proposal that interest should be charged on late payments.[4] **We agree with the proposal that payments to the UN's regular budget should be made on a quarterly basis rather than as a annual lump sum, and that under such a system it would be appropriate for interest to be charged on late payments.** Were these proposals to be implemented (and subsidiary suggestions such as increasing the level of the Working Capital Fund), the Independent Advisory Group concludes that the UN should not need to borrow either commercially or from the international institutions.

169. It has been argued that the system by which each Member State's assessment is calculated should be changed.[5] Currently a state's ability to pay is based on a ten-year average of its GNP, which has led to some anomalies. For instance, the figures for Russia are based on Soviet economic statistics which do not reflect current circumstances. The GNP of certain states has varied a great deal; Sir David Hannay pointed out that some of the Gulf countries pay "remarkably little" relatively speaking,[6] while the Advisory Committee note that much of eastern Asia has enjoyed fast economic growth in the last decade.[7] However, the FCO thought that the system was generally equitable and should not be changed.[8] The Advisory Committee recommends keeping the existing system but basing it on a three-year rather than a ten-year average of GNP.[9] **A three-year rather than a ten-year average of Member States' national income would provide a much fairer assessment of their ability to pay their contribution to the UN's budget. We recommend that the Government support this proposal in discussion of future UN financing.**

PAYING FOR PEACE-KEEPING

170. The cost of peace-keeping has increased fourfold since 1990–91. The UN spent an estimated $1.4 billion on peace-keeping in 1991–92, of which about half went on Cambodia.[10] The estimated amount of money the UN will spend on peace-keeping in 1992–93 is $3.827 billion, compared with $819 million in 1990–91. This enormous increase has led to the peace-keeping budget overtaking the regular budget. As the UN becomes more and more involved in peace-keeping operations, there is constant pressure for the money to be found; it is only because of large voluntary contributions made by countries such as Japan that some current operations have managed to scrape by.

---

[1] Ev.pp 249, 273.
[2] Q 53.
[3] *British Policy towards the United Nations*, Foreign Policy Document No.28, 1978.
[4] *Financing an Effective United Nations*, pp 9–10.
[5] eg. Ev.p 274.
[6] Q 53.
[7] *Financing an Effective United Nations*, p 13.
[8] Q 53.
[9] *op cit* p 14.
[10] *Financing an Effective United Nations*, pp 14–15.

171. Those of the Secretary-General's proposals in *An Agenda for Peace* which relate specifically to peace-keeping include establishing a peace-keeping reserve fund to cover the start-up costs of peace-keeping operations, a UN peace endowment fund of $1 billion, authorising the General Assembly to appropriate one-third of the estimated cost of each new peace-keeping operation as soon as the Security Council decides to establish an operation and authorising the Secretary-General to place contracts without the standard process of competitive tendering in exceptional circumstances.

172. The **peace endowment fund** met with no enthusiasm from FCO witnesses.[1] However, the **peace-keeping reserve fund** was welcomed by witnesses as a "genuinely useful" idea.[2] The idea of the fund, first suggested by Mr Perez de Cuellar, is to provide a pool of ready cash ($50 million) which could be used to meet initial expenses of peace-keeping operations.[3] It is clear from our inquiry that there is frequently too long a delay between the Security Council authorising action and deployment on the ground; much of this has been attributed to the cumbersome procedures used by the UN to finance peace-keeping operations. Sir David Hannay described the fund as a "start-up fund", designed to give the UN a kind of drawing capacity in the early stages of a peace-keeping operation. It is in this early stage that the need for payment is the most urgent; "it is often the moment at which the UN Secretariat need to be actually spending money on the transport of troops to the place which has been authorised, on getting equipment and so on". The money would be repaid into the fund from the usual assessed contributions when they come through; therefore the fund would be kept topped up.[4] During its 47th session (1992–93) the General Assembly, which has authority in budgetary matters, agreed to establish a start-up fund for peace-keeping costs, with a value of $150 million.[5] The Advisory Group believed that this was an important step, but that, given the "urgency, scope, danger and inherent unpredictability of peace-keeping", it should be much larger. To ensure that the UN is able to cover the start-up costs of several large missions, they believe the level of the fund should be raised to $400 million.[6] **We agree that, given the necessity for prompt deployment of peace-keeping operations, the United Nations peace-keeping reserve fund (or "start-up" fund) should be increased from $150 million to $400 million.**

173. The Advisory Group also suggest that the UN consider ending the funding of peace-keeping from ad hoc assessments each time a new operation is started and create a unified peace-keeping budget. The UN would submit an estimate for peace-keeping costs for the coming year, including an unappropriated margin to cover the start up costs of unexpected operations, and Member States would be asked to commit resources in advance rather than be called on at short notice throughout the year.[7] Such a unified budget would not only have advantages for the efficiency of running the operations, it would signal a recognition that peace-keeping was no longer to be regarded as an emergency measure but was a core activity of the Organisation. Mr Hogg told us that the UK government was satisfied with the ad hoc system of financing of UN peace-keeping operations.[8] While the UN only had to deal with a relatively small number of peace-keeping operations, the ad hoc system was satisfactory, it is no longer reasonable to expect it to function effectively in a world in which UN peace-keeping is no longer an emergency or exceptional activity. Therefore **we recommend that the Government support proposals to establish an annual peace-keeping assessment, perhaps payable (as we have suggested for the regular budget) on a quarterly basis.** This might enable the Government to make clearer to the House the actual cost of the UK's contribution to peace-keeping.

174. One other method of financing peace-keeping operations is significant: the voluntary financing of operations by participating parties such as the British contribution to the UNFICYP force in Cyprus. The contributors to the Bosnia UNPROFOR contingent, including the UK, originally paid for the deployment themselves. (The UK contribution is estimated at £100 million.[9]) Could the financial situation of UN peace-keeping be improved by further similar arrangements? There would clearly be an advantage as troops and backup would be available more quickly—Brigadier Harbottle suggested that the UK should set an example by bearing

---

[1] Q 134.
[2] Q 56.
[3] *An Agenda for Peace*, para 70(d).
[4] Q 56.
[5] *Financing an Effective United Nations*, p 18; also QQ 134–35.
[6] *Ibid* p 19.
[7] *Financing an Effective United Nations*.
[8] Q 135.
[9] Ev.p 3.

the costs of the participation of military/naval/air units or contingents for UN peace-keeping.[1] There is also a danger that letting Member States pay directly for their contributions to peace-keeping forces might lead to loss of control by the Secretary-General, and that the UN's authority might be compromised. It is interesting that the Secretary-General, after having asked participating states to shoulder the burden of UNPROFOR II in Bosnia directly themselves, has now changed his policy and wishes the whole of the UNPROFOR operation to be financed through the usual peace-keeping procedure. This is now the case (from the beginning of April 1993). However, an attempt by the Security Council to move to financing the Cyprus operation by means of the normal peace-keeping assessment, rather the present system of voluntary contributions, was vetoed by the Russian Federation on 11 May 1993. The Cyprus Government has now offered to meet a large proportion of the cost of the UN operation and on 27 June 1993 the Security Council agreed that the cost of that operation not covered by voluntary contributions should in future be financed by assessed contributions by Member States.[2]

175. The Secretary-General strongly supported proposals in some Member States that peace-keeping contributions should be financed from defence, rather than foreign affairs, budgets, because of the problems caused by the present volume and unpredictability of peace-keeping assessments.[3] Several of our witnesses supported this proposal. They argued that it would improve the payment record of Member States as defence budgets generally had more funds than foreign office budgets.[4] The Independent Advisory Group also suggested that Member States consider this option as contributions to UN peace-keeping were an investment in national security.[5] FCO and Ministry of Defence witnesses explained the rationale for the system used by the UK government for paying for UN peace-keeping operations. Military involvement in peace-keeping was in support of foreign policy objectives, and financial responsibility was aligned with policy responsibility. Therefore the initial expenditure connected with deploying the armed forces was charged to the Ministry of Defence, but the FCO reimbursed the Ministry of Defence for the amount.[6] The Foreign Secretary did not believe the question of which budget the money came from was of great importance. The question of finance would be of importance in deciding whether the UK became involved in a UN operation, but the decision would not revolve around which departmental budget the money came from.[7] If a Member State is unwilling to pay its peace-keeping dues, the difference between budgets is irrelevant; if unable to pay, the money will not be available from either budget. The question of whether the cost of peace-keeping comes from the Defence or FCO Votes is of peripheral importance compared to the primary decision as to whether a State wishes to contribute troops. **We consider it essential that the FCO is fully compensated through the public expenditure system for any unforeseen demands on its Vote arising out of peace-keeping policy decisions.** (We understand that the Defence Committee examined the implications of this question for the Ministry of Defence in its inquiry into UK Peace-keeping and Intervention Forces.)

176. There are arguments about the extent to which the UN's peace-keeping activities are hampered by lack of money; how far financial problems, as opposed to lack of political will or bureaucratic procedures, cause delay in the UN's reactions. As with other institutional reforms, creating new payment mechanisms may not be enough. The changes we suggest above should make it easier for states to make money available to the UN when it is needed, and could put the finances of the UN on a sounder footing. But, however efficient the UN's financing system becomes, **the proper funding of the Organisation will depend on Member States demonstrating their commitment to the UN by paying the contributions which are required of them by law.**

VII INSTITUTIONAL CHANGE

177. Given the expanding range and changing nature of the UN's mandate, there is obviously concern that the Organisation is efficient and sufficiently adaptable to meet the demands placed on it, and that it attracts and encourages staff of a high calibre. Equally, it must be representative of and accountable to all its Member States. In addressing these questions, the per-

---

[1] Ev.p 256.
[2] SCR 831.
[3] *An Agenda for Peace*, para 48
[4] eg. Dr Taylor, Brigadier Harbottle and the United Nations Association, Ev.pp 187, 256, 274.
[5] *Financing an Effective United Nations*, p 16
[6] Q 498.
[7] Ev.p 244, Q57.

formance of the General Assembly, the Security Council, the Secretariat and the various agencies have to be considered.

THE GENERAL ASSEMBLY

178. The General Assembly consists of all the members of the United Nations, and is the main deliberative organ of the Organisation. Although it has power to debate any matter within the scope of the Charter, only its recommendations relating to the internal affairs of the UN are binding. The Assembly's responsibilities include the election of the 10 non-permanent members of the Security Council and that of the Secretary-General (by a majority vote on the recommendation of the Security Council). The Assembly has ultimate authority in financial and budgetary matters.[1]

179. The Secretary-General has said that the moral authority of the UN depends on the full consultation and participation of all Member States.[2] The General Assembly is the forum in which such consultation and participation can best be expressed. In their memorandum, Christian Aid expressed concern that the reform process initiated by the Secretary-General had had the effect of augmenting the powers of the Security Council while reducing its accountability to the General Assembly.[3] Adding to the membership of the Council would not be enough; the relationship between the two should be reviewed.[4] Sir David Hannay denied that the Security Council had "usurped any of the privileges of the General Assembly".[5] The Assembly had to "develop and define its own rôle more than it has done up to now"; it was necessary to give the Assembly a more effective rôle but not at the expense of the Security Council. The FCO told us that the UK supported moves to "rationalise and streamline" the work of the Assembly in order to "revitalize" it.[6] During our visit to New York, the then President of the General Assembly, Mr Ganev, told us that the Assembly had established a working party on *Agenda for Peace* which would examine how the links between the Council and the Assembly could be improved so as to increase the UN's effectiveness. This is continuing its work, which may well bear fruit at the next session of the General Assembly.

THE SECURITY COUNCIL

180. The Security Council is the organ of the United Nations with primary responsibility for the maintenance of international peace and security. When it was founded in 1945, the United Nations had only 51 members, 11 of which were members of the Security Council. As the Organisation grew with decolonisation (more than 70 of the current members were colonies under foreign rule when the UN was created), the Council came to represent a smaller and smaller percentage of the membership. In 1965, when membership of the organisation had reached 118, the Security Council was enlarged from 11 to 15 members, though the permanent membership remained unchanged. Since then the UN has gained another 63 members, over twenty of which have joined in the present decade. Membership now stands at 183.

181. Five of the Security Council members are permanent—China, France, the Russian Federation, the United Kingdom and the United States.[7] The other 10, representing important regional groupings in the United Nations, are non-permanent, elected by the General Assembly for two year terms on a staggered basis—five one year, five another. Thus the composition of the Council changes each year.[8] The Security Council takes decisions on behalf of all the members of the United Nations. Substantive decisions require nine votes out of 15. These must include the concurring votes of the permanent members. In practice, however, concurrence includes not only a positive vote but also abstention, not participating in the vote and absence. If a permanent member casts a negative vote, i.e. it uses its veto, it prevents the Security Council from acting. The veto does not apply to procedural questions.

---

[1] Charter, Article 17.
[2] *Annual Report*,para 169.
[3] Ev.p 301.
[4] *Ibid* para 12.
[5] Q 29.
[6] Ev.p 3.
[7] The General Assembly agreed in 1971 that China should be represented by the People's Republic of China rather than by the Republic of China (Taiwan); in 1991 the Russian Federation was recognised as the successor state to the USSR.
[8] The current non-permanent members are Brazil, Cape Verde, Djibouti, Hungary, Japan, Morocco, New Zealand, Pakistan, Venezuela and Spain.

182. During our inquiry **the composition of the Security Council**, and whether it is appropriate for the 1990s, has been raised. In particular, there have been calls for Germany and Japan to be given permanent membership, for example by President Clinton during his election campaign and more recently by the US Permanent Representative to the UN.[1] During our visit to New York, we had the benefit of discussing the subject with the Permanent Representative of Japan and the representative of Indonesia (current president of the Non-Aligned Movement), as well as with the representatives of several permanent members. While in New York we also heard that the new spirit of cooperation between the permanent members of the Security Council was causing concern among non-members, who feared that it was becoming a ratifying chamber which rubber-stamped the decisions of the permanent five.[2]

183. The principal argument for altering or increasing the permanent membership of the Council is that it is out of date and therefore unrepresentative: it is a product of the Second World War and "does not reflect the economic, political and military realities of the 1990s".[3] Witnesses argued that, if the Council were to act on behalf of all Member States it needed more equitable geographical representation; unless the UN were better able to represent the world's states, confidence in the organisation would evaporate, particularly in the South.[4] During our visit to the UN, Japan, Germany, India, Pakistan, Indonesia, Egypt, Nigeria and Brazil were all mentioned as being possible candidates for permanent membership. A former British Permanent Representative to the UN, Sir Anthony Parsons, has proposed that five permanent members should be added to the Council, bringing its numbers up to 20: these additional members should be Germany and Japan, together with one seat each for a representative country from Africa, Latin America and Asia. He admits that this would create a more "unwieldy" Council, but argues this would not be unreasonable given that the membership of the Organisation has expanded from 50 to nearer two hundred countries.[5] The French Government has argued that permanent membership should be confined to nuclear powers.

184. We heard a good deal of evidence against changing the composition of the Council at the present time. For the first time since 1945, it was argued, the Security Council had begun to operate as it was intended to operate and it would be a mistake to try and change it now.[6] The Foreign Secretary was not persuaded of the need for reform, arguing that it would create more controversy at a time when it was performing well.[7] As one witness put it, such "musical chairs" would be a "wasteful diversion of energy".[8] The permanent members need to be able to operate as an efficient executive body with the capacity for crisis management at all times. Lord Gladwyn, who as one of the original drafters of the Charter has a special locus in this matter, agreed that the present system was out of date but told us that a larger Council, as suggested by Sir Anthony Parsons, would be "so unwieldy as to be inoperable". Divisionism would be more rather than less common in the post-Cold War world and an effective Security Council was therefore needed even more.[9] Sir Crispin Tickell believed that 15 was the "golden number" of members; any more would reduce the Council's effectiveness.[10]

185. The countries most frequently proposed as additional permanent members are Japan and Germany, most notably because of their economic status: they contribute 12.45% and 8.93% respectively of the UN's regular budget, compared to the USA's 25% and the UK's 5.02 %.[11] Japan has also contributed nearly half of the non-peace-keeping costs of the UN's operation in Cambodia. The economic power of Germany and Japan is recognised by their membership of the G7. Mr Hogg told us that, while he understood the argument that paying the piper involved some share in calling the tune, he did not believe that there was any natural correlation between economic weight and permanent membership of the Security Council.[12] Some witnesses argued that to claim that Japan, Germany and other Member States were

[1] Ev.p 308 ftn; see also Q 157.
[2] See also Ev.p 184; QQ 361,366.
[3] Ev.pp 252, 275–276.
[4] Ev.pp 300–301.
[5] *International Relations*, December 1992 p 200; summarised in Ev.p 262.
[6] Q 25.
[7] Ev.12 October 1992, Q 64.
[8] Ev.p 251.
[9] Ev.p 326.
[10] Q 366.
[11] Ev.pp 72–75.
[12] QQ 162,157.

excluded from decisions because they did not have permanent membership was an oversimplification.[1] In practice, the permanent members of the Security Council took account of the views of other members (for instance, in the discussion over Namibia) more than was commonly realised.[2] Mr Hogg also told us that the UK was very sensitive to the views of other EC Member States, discussed matters with them and represented their views on the Council.[3]

186. The main arguments for **abolishing the veto** are that the veto gives undue weight to the permanent five members of the Council and that decisions are reached on the basis of trying to avoid vetoes. Christian Aid and the United Nations Association argued that the existence of the veto was an "injustice" and prevented the Organisation from being properly accountable to its members.[4] The Secretary-General has stated that during the Cold War the UN was "rendered powerless ... because of the vetoes—279 of them—cast in the Security Council, which were a vivid expression of the divisions of that period".[5] Professor Roberts notes that the veto is "widely perceived as having held the UN back from fulfilling its functions in the Cold War years" but is not convinced by the Secretary-General's analysis.[6]

187. Some witnesses were in favour of keeping the veto power. Sir John Thomson argued that in the past, use of the veto stopped the UN from getting involved in situations which it would have been unable to solve.[7] Its existence had also ensured that both the US and USSR remained members of the UN during the Cold War; it had been "an essential part of ... achieving collective security" in the past and was still indispensable to the effectiveness of the Council.[8] Sir David Hannay commented that the veto was now being used properly, rather than for ideological reasons; this weakened the argument for abolishing it.[9] Professor Roberts cautioned against the assumption in *An Agenda for Peace* that the era of the veto was over,[10] and the Foreign Secretary was not keen for the UK to lose the veto power.[11] The recent use of the veto by the Russian Federation on 11 May 1993 in a vote on the funding of the Cyprus operation is a reminder that the new-found unity of the permanent five cannot be taken for granted. It is not yet clear whether this use of the veto is a one-off abberation or sets the pattern for future practice in the Security Council. **We do not believe that it is practical to expect the permanent members of the Security Council as presently constituted to give up their right to the veto.**

188. Changing the size of the Council or amending the veto provisions would require amendment of the Charter. This requires a two-thirds majority of the General Assembly and the agreement of all the permanent members of the Security Council. Witnesses pointed out the improbability of the Assembly managing to agree on new members and veto powers. Sir David Hannay stated that there would be no possibility of the General Assembly agreeing to add Japan and Germany alone,[12] and Sir John Thomson pointed out there was a wide range of other candidates: it was difficult to see which would get the required majority.[13] **Although there are strong arguments for and against enlarging the Security Council we do not consider it likely that the General Assembly would agree to give Japan and Germany permanent membership of the Security Council without giving it to other states; obtaining agreement within the membership on the identity of those states is likely to be extremely difficult.**

189. **It is clear that the debate over the composition of the Council will continue and the UK must be prepared to take a constructive approach to it**; the Foreign Secretary told us that the UK had no wish to stifle the debate.[14] If the Council's composition is to remain unchanged, the permanent members must ensure that they keep the confidence of other Member States. The regular consultations with other EC members by France and the United Kingdom should

---

[1] QQ 363-64; also the Foreign Secretary, Ev.p 232 (Q 64).
[2] Q 366.
[3] Q 157.
[4] Ev.p 251, 301.
[5] *An Agenda for Peace*, para 14.
[6] Ev.p 308.
[7] Q 362.
[8] Q 362.
[9] Q 26.
[10] Ev.p 308.
[11] Q 64.
[12] Q 24.
[13] QQ 361,362,367; also Ev.p 308.
[14] QQ 361.

be continued and consultation with other Member States should be developed further. The need for the Security Council to retain the full support of the membership is particularly evident when authorising military action. Given the difficulties inherent in attempting to change the composition of the Security Council, ways should be sought to involve other Member States in the decision-making process relating to peace-keeping and other military activity. **The regular meetings of the so-called "core group"—the permanent five plus states with a particular involvement in financing, or contributing forces to, an operation—are a welcome development. They allow the permanent five members to undertake the fullest consultation with the other key countries in any operation without the effectiveness of the Security Council's decision-making capacity being impaired. This allows Member States who contribute financially and logistically, especially to the UN's ever-increasing military rôle, to have a more powerful voice in the ways in which military force is employed, while avoiding the need for potentially divisive changes to the UN Charter.**

190. The FCO has put forward a number of arguments for **retaining the United Kingdom's permanent seat** on the Security Council; they are set out at length in their memorandum.[1] The FCO's basic argument—that British permanent membership is good not only for the UK but for the UN itself—has not altered from the evidence given to the Committee by the then Foreign Secretary in 1980.[2] **Whether or not changes are made to the composition of the Security Council the FCO told us that there is no pressure for Britain to give up its permanent membership[3] and our impression from visits and the balance of evidence received tends to confirm this.**

THE SECRETARY-GENERAL, THE SECRETARIAT AND THE AGENCIES

191. The part played by the Secretary-General is crucial to the success of the UN's work. Although we took little evidence specifically on his rôle, a number of witnesses drew attention to the ways in which he influences events. For instance, our adviser, Mr Travers, describes the ways in which the Secretary-General can alert the Security Council to potential crises in world affairs[4] and the FCO among others have stressed the importance of his authority in this field. He has many other tasks and has been described as holding "three or four more or less full-time jobs".[5] They include the administration and management of the Secretariat, the coordination of the UN system, official representation of the UN around the world, crisis management and the maintenance of a global watch on areas of potential crisis. **Given the range of tasks expected of him, the choice of Secretary-General, and the support (logistical and political) he receives are both absolutely crucial.**

192. The position of the Secretary-General embodies many of the tensions and difficulties facing the UN as a whole. He is expected to cope with a daunting range and number of tasks; he is expected both to be an impartial mediator and where necessary an activist; and a guardian of peace who has to organise and run a large number of military operations. One witness noted that as the UN becomes more "activist", the tensions at the heart of the Secretary-General's job could become more acute.[6] It is extraordinary however that there is no provision in the Charter for anyone to deputise or stand in for the Secretary-General if he is ill or otherwise unable to take decisions. When we met the present Secretary-General in New York, we were impressed by his energetic commitment both to the administrative reform of the Organisation and to exploiting to the full the opportunities afforded by the end of the Cold War to "achieve the great objectives of the Charter".[7] Even if and perhaps especially if, the prospect of a "new spirit of commonality" which he describes in *An Agenda for Peace* fades away in the face of renewed conflict among the international community, the Secretary-General deserves and requires the support of all Member States. **Consideration should be given to greater delegation by the Secretary-General of some of his tasks, perhaps by the appointment of a deputy Secretary-General to share the burden.**

193. There has long been a perception that, whatever the UN might have achieved in fields such as peace-keeping or humanitarian relief, it has suffered from many of the faults of any

---

[1] Ev.pp 321–323.
[2] Foreign and Commonwealth Office Organisation, Second Report of the Foreign Affairs Committee, HC 511 1979–80, QQ 312–14.
[3] Ev.p 322.
[4] Ev.p 336ff.
[5] Brian Urquhart and Erskine Childers, *A World in Need of Leadership*, p 38.
[6] Ev.p 259.
[7] *An Agenda for Peace*, para 3.

bureaucracy. The comments CARE made to us were perhaps typical of this view: the UN was "a large and unwieldy bureaucracy" which was "incredibly expensive". Any multinational company facing its shareholders with similar problems probably would have called in management consultants many years ago.[1] Since coming into office the Secretary-General has made efforts to streamline the Secretariat and is now intent on extending this reorganisation to other parts of the United Nations system.[2] It is his intention to focus the work of the UN "on the field, the locations where economic, social and political decisions take effect".[3]

194. Streamlining the Secretariat has so far involved abolishing 12 offices and departments and 14 high level posts, including Under-Secretary General posts where these were not regarded as necessary. Lines of communication have been clarified and duplication of effort reduced.[4] In the next phase of reform, the Secretary-General intends to concentrate on other parts of the UN system, in particular to improve the coordination of the work of the specialised agencies.[5] The Security Council recently encouraged "coordinated action by other components of the United Nations system to remedy the underlying causes of threat to peace and security".[6]

195. The UK government has been supportive of the Secretary-General's programme of reform. Sir David Hannay regarded the UN's essential problem as the gradual growth of the organisation without clear enough priorities and objectives. Under-Secretary General posts had grown over the years with no clear definition of their functions. There were overlaps and unnecessary offices lower down the system too.[7] He told us that the initial efforts of the Secretary-General had been "admirable" and a more "coherent structure" was emerging in the Secretariat. The Government were now encouraging him to follow through the rationalisation process in the rest of the UN system. The priorities of the UN had to be changed to reflect its changing rôle: more attention had to be given to higher priorities such as peace-keeping, human rights and humanitarian affairs. This would not be easy as international organisations were less adaptable to changing priorities than national governments.[8] Professor Higgins suggested wholesale abolition of some UN organs to release funding for higher priority areas such as human rights.[9] Dr Taylor quoted an American official: the part of the secretariat dealing with peace-keeping was "a corner grocery shop undertaking"—more resources needed to be directed to it.[10]

196. We were told that reorganising the agencies and their relationship with the Secretariat would be difficult. Sir David Hannay pointed out that each agency had its own constitution and structure and agencies were not the servants of the Secretary-General.[11] The Secretary-General lays great store by the work of the Administrative Committee on Coordination (ACC), whose members include the executive heads of all the specialised agencies and organisations of the UN, and he has commissioned a study by management consultants of ways in which it can be made more effective.[12] Sir David noted that making the Committee a more effective and policy-orientated body was "definitely an up-hill task" but one that deserved support.[13] Sir John Thomson was not encouraging about the ACC: although it had the potential to bring agencies together and to provide an opportunity for the Secretary-General to "bang heads together", in his experience at the UN "it was perfectly pathetic and the Secretary-General barely had the power to propose what time they were going to meet in the afternoon". However, he noted that the power for better coordination was there and should be exercised.[14]

---

[1] Ev.p 29; Q 97.
[2] Annual Report, para 23–29.
[3] *An Agenda for Peace*, para 83.
[4] Ev.p 3, 32, Q 20, Annual Report pp 9–10.
[5] Annual Report p 13, QQ 20–21. Strictly speaking, some of the best-known UN institutions, such as the UNHCR and UNDP, are not specialised agencies under the terms of the UN's constitution. However, for the sake of simplicity, they and the other subsidiary institutions of the UN are referred to as "agencies" throughout our Report.
[6] Note by the President of the Security Council, 30 April 1993.
[7] Q 20.
[8] Q 22; Ev.p 3; also Q 163.
[9] Ev.p 180, Q 409. Professor Higgins suggested the following could be wound up: the Special Committee against Apartheid, the Commission against Apartheid in Sports, the Committee on the Exercise of Inalienable Rights of Palestinian People and various regional and regional economic commissions within the UN.
[10] Ev.p 186.
[11] Q 20.
[12] Annual Report pp 11–13.
[13] Q 20.
[14] Q 359.

197. FCO officials agreed that any approach to reorganising the structure and work of the specialised agencies had to be "agency-specific": there was no "global approach" that could be allocated to all of them. Member States had a responsibility to encourage reform within individual agencies.[1] However, governments should not try to "micro-manage" the Secretary-General or go along with blueprints for what he should do. "In the end he has to manage it for himself".[2]

198. **We agree with the view expressed by non-governmental organisations that more devolved responsibility is needed within the UN system, which is "over-centralised and bureaucratic".**[3] They told us that the Secretary-General's Special Representative should be given authority to make on-the-ground decisions without reference to New York.[4] This extended to the agencies: in the World Food Programme, there was "often a low level of field autonomy, with management imposed from headquarters" (although this was starting to improve).[5] **We agree with Baroness Chalker that efforts to reform the agencies should be concentrated on ensuring that there is "more work at the coalface and perhaps less in the boardroom".**[6]

INSTITUTIONAL ASPECTS OF THE UN'S HUMANITARIAN RESPONSE

199. The work of the UN in the field of humanitarian relief provides a good example of the Organisation's institutional problems. Two **problems of coordination** emerged from our inquiry: coordination within the UN itself (the agencies and the Secretariat) and a perceived lack of effective cooperation between the UN and other humanitarian organisations. It was argued that the UN took too long to get involved in some crises and there was also a perception that, once involved, the relief efforts of the UN were often weakened by duplication and rivalry.[7] The lack of a single figure of authority in UN operations was also raised; in Somalia, for instance, different coordinators and special representatives were appointed, causing confusion among workers on the ground.[8] At its best the UN has successfully performed remarkable tasks in the field. The UNHCR has relieved the situation of refugees in the former Yugoslavia, and in Cambodia, it achieved a magnificent feat of organisation and logistics in the repatriation of more than 350,000 refugees from Thailand. During our visit to Cambodia we were enormously impressed by the success of this undertaking, which has been cited even by some critics of the UNTAC operation as a credit to the UN. The task for the UN is to replicate this kind of success elsewhere in the system.

The Department for Humanitarian Affairs

200. One of the ways by which it was hoped to improve the coordination of the humanitarian effort between the specialised agencies was the establishment in March 1992, on the initiative of the UK and Germany, of the Department of Humanitarian Affairs (DHA). The UN's response to the crisis of the Iraqi Kurds in 1991 gave a fresh impetus to attempts to create a new and more effective body to coordinate humanitarian activities. The UK, together with Germany, launched the initiative which eventually led to the passing of General Assembly Resolution 46/182 on 19 December 1991. This resolution, entitled "Strengthening of the coordination of humanitarian emergency assistance of the United Nations", formed the basis of the new department and the post of Under Secretary-General for Humanitarian Affairs. The DHA is charged with coordinating the work of the various relief agencies within the UN system[9]; the Foreign Secretary cited it as an example of the way the Secretary-General was trying to tighten and improve his control over the UN's agencies.[10]

201. Many witnesses did not believe the DHA was working as intended. Witnesses listed a number of reasons for its shortcomings. It had a "derisory" budget; the head of the DHA did not have the status to control the heads of agencies and had no financial control over them; and the organisation suffered from being based in two places.[11] Baroness Chalker told us that the DHA was not intended to be imposed on the UN agencies or to control them, but to coor-

---

[1] Q 164.
[2] Q 21.
[3] Ev.p 28.
[4] Ev.pp 28,37.
[5] Ev.p 29.
[6] Q 331.
[7] eg. Ev.p 119.
[8] Ev.p 37.
[9] Ev.pp 150,296; Q 329.
[10] Q 290.
[11] Ev.pp 119,290.

dinate and facilitate their work.[1] The ODA stated that there were often "sound operational reasons" for giving an individual agency a leading rôle in a particular case.[2] Generally, while the NGOs were wary of the UN controlling their activities under the guise of coordination, they were keen to see the DHA having greater control over the UN's humanitarian operations.

202. The rôle and authority of the DHA was "still unclear", according to Save the Children.[3] This lack of clarity was evident on the ground; the Development Studies Association noted that in Somalia the DHA deployed staff on the ground in addition to the UN's Resident Representative.[4] Not all the UN's agencies were cooperating properly with the DHA.[5] Save the Children pointed out that almost as soon as it was established, its head, Mr Eliasson, was despatched on a round of visits to international trouble spots, when a better investment of time might have been to concentrate on the detailed planning of the DHA.[6] Baroness Chalker also told us that Mr Eliasson had become "an international humanitarian trouble shooter", leaving him less time to get involved in coordination issues.[7] Witnesses were agreed that the DHA should not become another *operational* agency. Mr Sahnoun told us that it should not be an agency with branches everywhere. Its head should be like an orchestral conductor, not trying to play all the instruments and believing he plays them better than others, but persuading the instrumentalists to play in harmony.[8]

203. Doubts were raised as to how effectively the DHA could operate given the division of its offices between New York and Geneva. Save the Children stated that the division was "particularly damaging" to its effectiveness. It undermined good administration, divided scarce resources and artificially separated the political and operational functions of the Department. The impetus to divide it had in Save the Children's opinion come from donor governments; they were unconvinced that their arguments outweighed the case for unified control.[9] The British Red Cross believed that the DHA should be based entirely in Geneva, as it needed to be "in amongst the key agencies" working in the field.[10] Baroness Chalker, in her speech to the General Assembly, argued that for "complex political emergencies with political dimensions, policy coordination should be concentrated in New York, while operational coordination should rest in Geneva where the institutional expertise was located".[11] She told us that the division of labour, if properly used, could be effective, although communications between the two had to be "first rate".[12]

204. Baroness Chalker has stated that the DHA's creation was never intended to be an instant or complete solution.[13] She agreed that it had had problems over staff, administrative support and resources. An internal UN review is being conducted into the work of the DHA which she hoped would find solutions to its problems.[14] Witnesses made a number of recommendations to us as to how its performance could be improved. It should have stronger powers over the functions of other UN agencies in humanitarian crises.[15] Its head should have financial control over the actions of the agencies and in extreme cases operational control.[16] Its budget needed to be increased;[17] it needed to have more control over the UN's funds for relief generally[18] and specifically, it should have control over how extra funds voted for specific disaster situations are allocated between different agencies.[19] Finally, it should be located on one site, in Geneva.[20] Many of the suggestions put forward by witnesses for improving he DHA are not possible to implement, given the constitutional independence of the agencies—the

[1] Q330.
[2] Ev.p 150.
[3] Ev.p 38.
[4] Ev.p 290.
[5] Ev.p 32; Red Cross Q 224.
[6] Ev.p 38.
[7] Q 329.
[8] Q 447.
[9] Ev.p 38.
[10] Q 224.
[11] Statement to the 47th Session of the UN General Assembly, 20 November 1992.
[12] QQ 329–30.
[13] Statement to the 47th Session of the UN General Assembly, 20 November 1992.
[14] Q 329.
[15] Ev.p 32.
[16] Ev.p 292.
[17] Q 224,228; Ev.p 292.
[18] Q 228.
[19] Ev.p 119.
[20] *Ibid*, also Ev.p 38.

Secretary-General cannot by personal fiat make them obey the instructions of the head of the DHA. **The Department of Humanitarian Affairs has not yet been able to fulfil the intentions behind its establishment to improve the UN's coordination of its emergency response. It has been in existence for little more than a year. It is too early to pass judgement on its performance.**

UN interim offices

205. Given these difficulties, it may be that the way ahead for the UN to coordinate its response to complex emergencies lies in the expansion of UN Interim Offices, bringing together UN agencies in the field under one roof, such as have been established in the former Soviet Union.[1] These missions carry out a mixture of humanitarian and political functions, the emphasis of which changes depending on the circumstances.[2] Offices of this kind could help promote a more adaptable attitude of mind among the different elements of the UN system. It may be easier to start such new ventures in areas which have never had a UN presence before, but these efforts should be borne in mind as a possible model for the future. **We consider that the Secretary-General should be given full support in his effort to develop the concept of interim UN offices where the organisation of all UN personnel in a country can be brought together.**

206. **In considering how best to improve the UN's humanitarian response, an *ad hoc* approach is inevitable: every crisis is unique. The key for the UN as far as organisational effectiveness is concerned is to find the most appropriate postholder or lead agency and give it overall command.** This might for instance be UNHCR (as in Bosnia)[3], or the Secretary-General's Special Representative (as in the case of UNTAC in Cambodia). Mr Sahnoun described what he regarded as the ideal model for exercising the UN's authority in the field, based on his experience in Somalia. Although there had to be a figure on the ground with political authority, who was the focus for the UN operation, below him there needed to be a manager of the day-to-day activities of the UN. One person could not do both. A coordinator of humanitarian assistance alone would not have the same authority as the Special Representative, while the Special Representative would not have the time to act as a day-to-day manager.[4] (The importance of devolved authority was stressed by Save the Children among others).[5]

Cooperation with other humanitarian organisations

207. **Effective cooperation between the UN and other humanitarian organisations is as important as that between the UN agencies themselves.** The UN has worked for many years in humanitarian operations in conjunction with NGOs and ideally each would benefit from the experience of the other's expertise. However, their relationship has frequently been difficult, and many of those who gave us evidence, or whom we met on our visits, stressed that a better *modus vivendi* needed to be found. Mr Sahnoun, for instance, told us that

> "more and more reliance on the NGOs should be perceived as positive on the part of the United Nations agencies, not as competition ... the UN should recognise ... the rôle of the NGOs, respect it, give it a higher status, co-ordinate with them as much as possible and help them. I think there should not be opposition in the perception of their work, they should see each other as complementary."[6]

The UN could be most helpful by providing an "umbrella" under which different organisations could work.[7] Mr Sahnoun thought there might even be a written contract allocating a division of labour between the UN, whose principal job was to provide logistical support to the relief effort, and the NGOs, which by their nature were more flexible and decentralised.[8] CARE told us that this kind of flexibility, allowing for a more rapid response to changing situations, was being practised by UNHCR in Iraq.[9]

208. The British Red Cross told us that "increased cooperation between the many humanitarian players presently active on the scene of emergencies is an obvious need".[10] Cooperation

---

[1] *Annual Report* p 11; Ev.p 359.
[2] Ev.p 359.
[3] Q 314.
[4] QQ 429,431,447.
[5] Ev.p 37.
[6] QQ 435,438.
[7] *Ibid.*
[8] Q 435.
[9] Ev.p 29.
[10] Ev.p 118.

should include all the organisations, not least because large-scale interventions by government agencies often had to be implemented on the ground by voluntary bodies.[1] Mr Sahnoun told us that he had experienced problems with the relationship between the ICRC and one of the UN agencies in Somalia: "they were fighting each other because they considered they each had the same constituency with other donor countries". Such rivalry between organisations could be very damaging; in some cases they were attempting to outbid each other in hiring local staff or accommodation.[2] We heard of at least one other turf war during our visit to Somalia, which, while it had been resolved, had obviously created bad feeling between different organisations and had done no good for the relief effort. In Somalia, members of the Committee heard various complaints from representatives of humanitarian relief organisations about the shortcomings of the UN. We also heard rebuttals of these from UN staff. It is not possible for us to determine who in each case was right or wrong, but it was obvious that improvement in communications and coordination of effort between the different actors could only improve matters.

209. Witnesses were concerned that the UN should be a helper of others as much as an operational organisation in its own right. Baroness Chalker told us that, while NGOs often needed coordination by the UN, especially in a war zone, they did not want to be *controlled* by the UN. NGOs should be involved whenever their participation would be of benefit—they were often the best vehicles by which to deliver aid and the UN should utilise them.[3] Save the Children stressed that the UN "do not have to do everything".[4] The British Red Cross were concerned that, because of pressure from government and the media, the UN would try to get more and more involved in the operational part of the delivery of relief aid, which would detract from the work that the UN could do best and which only the UN could do, such as peace-keeping.[5] UN workers in Mogadishu told members of the Committee that the UN had an important rôle in providing government and security structures where these were weak or non-existent, and providing funding for NGO projects where this was most appropriate. The NGOs were perhaps best at short-term crisis-management, but this was changing—for instance Save the Children (UK) was to rehabilitate irrigation canals in Somalia on behalf of the UNDP.

210. A common complaint throughout our inquiry was that the UN failed to respond swiftly and adequately to humanitarian crises. It is debatable how far this is due to administrative or organisational failings. Witnesses such as Mr Sahnoun thought it was due in part to problems inherent in the UN system,[6] but political will (or the lack of it) among Member States was crucial. The UN system needs to keep itself informed of potential crises on the humanitarian front as much as in the field of conflict (as discussed in para 47 above). To this end, it was put to us by witnesses that the UN should make more use of non-official sources of information at the preventive stage, before crises developed. NGOs working in affected countries could often provide a level of expert knowledge which the UN did not possess. In Cambodia, for instance, members of the Committee were told that the UN mine-clearing operation relied initially on maps produced by a British NGO, the Halo Trust (which is also involved directly in mine-clearing operations) and members of the Committee were told that in Bosnia the UN relief operation initially acquired maps and information from Medecins Sans Frontières. Baroness Chalker suggested that the UN could rely more on assessments from other organisations.[7] The Development Studies Association cited evidence which suggested that, in Mozambique, the UN was reluctant to use information provided by NGOs.[8] NGOs told us that the DHA needed to build up a capacity to make strategic analyses of information, enabling the UN to act more quickly to avert humanitarian crises.[9] This is as important a part of preventive diplomacy as the various early warning mechanisms discussed in paras 41–60 above. **Early warning of potential humanitarian disasters, in which organisations outside the UN have an important part to play, should enable the UN to become involved sooner in situations which also frequently have serious implications for international peace and security.**

---

[1] Ev.p 119.
[2] Q 434.
[3] QQ 334–37.
[4] Q 72.
[5] Q 215.
[6] Q 419.
[7] Q 336.
[8] Ev.p 292.
[9] QQ 77–78.

STAFFING QUESTIONS

211. The UN's huge and ever-increasing range of tasks demand more than merely institutional improvement. The UN Charter stipulates that

> "the paramount consideration in the employment of staff and in the determination of the conditions of service shall be the necessity of securing the highest standards of efficiency, competence and integrity ."[1]

The Secretary-General is also enjoined to pay "due regard" to the importance of recruiting staff on a wide geographical basis. This is reflected in the allocation of certain posts to particular countries or groupings of countries. For instance, when the UN was first established, a 'gentleman's agreement' ensured that five Assistant Secretary-General posts were reserved for nationals of the permanent members of the Security Council.[2]

212. During our visits to the UN's headquarters and to its operations in various parts of the world we met many UN staff who impressed us by their enthusiasm and commitment, often in very difficult circumstances. In Cambodia and the former Yugoslavia, individual UN employees were performing remarkable feats of organisation, mediation, rehabilitation and assistance. There are also some outstanding people working in the higher echelons of the UN. However, concern was expressed throughout our inquiry about the way in which staff, both in the field and in the headquarters bureaucracy, were selected and how they performed their duties.

213. Several witnesses commented on the calibre of UN staff. CARE argued that one of the UN's problems was the calibre of staff deployed, particularly overseas, by the UN agencies.[3] Dr Prins referred to the "the fudge which has for many years filled the UN administration with representative quotas of less than optimally efficient administrators".[4] OXFAM argued that failure of the UN in Somalia, for instance, was in part due to the appointment of staff not according to ability but according to the "internal politics of the UN"—having to fulfil quotas for different nationalities rather than getting the right person for the job.[5] Mr Sahnoun made similar comments: during the Cold War governments had pressurised the UN to hire certain people, rather than letting the Secretariat find the best people.[6] While in New York, we were told that the nature of the Organisation's personnel management had also contributed to lower staff quality. The calibre of staff is a problem not only in the field of humanitarian relief; Professor Groom pointed out that if the UN is to become more proactive in the prevention of conflict, new skills will be needed of staff.[7] The Secretary-General also calls for more training of non-military peace-keeping personnel, such as police.[8]

214. There was a perception among some witnesses that the UN system, as a large bureaucracy, tended to attract and promote the wrong kind of person. Mr Sahnoun commented that many UN personnel had not been recruited for the kinds of job they were now expected to do; they had expected "some kind of prestige position" and were not always prepared to put up with poor accommodation or insecure situations.[9] The staff of NGOs often showed a greater commitment and dynamism than those of the UN.[10] There was also a need to appoint the right kind of people at the top of the Organisation. For instance, the British Red Cross, while not passing any personal judgement on the current head of the DHA, argued that the DHA needed a manager in charge rather than a diplomat, given the nature of his task.[11] The British Red Cross also implied that their own operations tended to be more cost effective because their staff salaries were not as high as those of the UN.[12] Members were told by NGO staff in Somalia that excessive UN allowances and costs appeared not to be related to local conditions. In Cambodia members of the Committee learned of resentment at the high level of UN salaries.

---

[1] Article 101.
[2] Urquhart and Childers, *A World in Need of Leadership* p 37.
[3] Q 100.
[4] Ev.p 250.
[5] Q 79.
[6] QQ 420,441–42.
[7] Ev.p 259.
[8] *An Agenda for Peace*, para 52.
[9] Q 420.
[10] *Ibid.*
[11] Q 224.
[12] Q 215.

215. CARE suggested that improvement in the field of humanitarian and development work could be achieved by greater rotation of staff between the field and headquarters,[1] which NGOs have generally found beneficial. The Secretary-General is also encouraging it; for instance, the Special Representative in Cambodia was formerly Under-Secretary General for Disarmament Affairs and many of UNTAC's personnel were drawn from New York headquarters. While in principle this is a good idea, and would obviously improve the experience of staff members, it could in fact go against the ideal of appointing the best staff for the job in hand.[2] It was put to us in Somalia that too rapid a turnover of staff in both NGOs and the UN had sometimes hampered efforts at better cooperation.

216. Mr Sahnoun argued that the UN needed a wholesale restaffing with people who were prepared to face the rigours of work in the field rather than those who had come into the organisation for a comfortable career. While this was taking place, much of the UN's relief work could be done by people seconded from NGOs[3] Even if his approach were not adopted, there may be lessons for the UN to learn from the more flexible, devolved personnel management structures of the non-governmental relief organisations. Another possibility is to encourage "outsiders" to come and work for the Organisation in mid-career, rather than relying on personnel who have spent their entire working lives in the UN. When in Geneva we were told that the DHA was building up a rapid response system, by which civil servants from Member States could be brought in on a contract basis to carry out specific urgent tasks. During our visit to the former Yugoslavia, we met a UN worker who joined the organisation after a career in documentary television. Such **appointments from outside the UN career service might bring fresh thinking into the Organisation and encourage cultural change. We agree with the local representative of a UN agency in Somalia who told members that the UN needed to break some of its traditional conventions and learn new ways of working. We recommend that where appropriate the UN should utilise relevant expertise to do more of the liaison work currently done by full-time UN employees.**

An international criminal court

217. One of the ways in which it has long been suggested that the UN could help defeat breaches of international humanitarian law is the establishment of an international criminal court, which would have the power to try those accused of such violations. There have been suggestions (going back to 1948)[4] for a permanent international criminal court. Professor Higgins favoured this approach, while pointing out that under international law any state could try itself persons accused of war crimes. A standing court would not be seen as administering "victors' justice" in the way either an *ad hoc* tribunal or a single state or group of states might.[5] The International Law Commission is currently examining the creation of such a permanent international court,[6] which would require a General Assembly mandate.

218. Throughout the crisis in the former Yugoslavia, there have been calls for the establishment of a separate tribunal to try those accused of "war crimes" in the region. Lord Owen and Mr Cyrus Vance have recommended establishing an international criminal court for those accused of war crimes in former Yugoslavia.[7] There were calls after the Gulf War to try Saddam Hussein for similar crimes. Under Security Council Resolution 808, the UN has established an *ad hoc* tribunal to try persons accused of violations of the Geneva Conventions and other branches of international humanitarian law in the former Yugoslavia. A Commission of experts meeting in Geneva is examining allegations of breaches of humanitarian law, mass killings and other atrocities in the former Yugoslavia.

219. Lord Owen told the Committee that the advantage of an *ad hoc* tribunal was that it could be set up relatively quickly, whereas a standing international court needing General Assembly approval would take longer to establish and opportunities to try alleged war criminals would be missed.[8] The British Red Cross, while welcoming the adoption by the Security Council of Resolution 780 (which established the commission of experts on a tribunal for for-

---

[1] Q 100.
[2] *Ibid.*
[3] Q 441–42.
[4] Ev.p 315.
[5] Q 415–16.
[6] Q 416; Ev.pp 328–9.
[7] *Ibid.*
[8] Q 189.

mer Yugoslavia), doubted whether states would go further and agree to accept the jurisdiction of a permanent international criminal court.[1] Mr Hogg has said that there are "substantial legal, political and practical obstacles "to establishing such a court.[2]

220. One obvious argument against establishing a tribunal for former Yugoslavia is that it would be selective: if Bosnia, why not Iraq or Cambodia? A standing court would not be seen as discriminatory[3] and would reflect the Organisation's universality. However, in this as in other areas of the UN's activity, a pragmatic approach may have to be adopted. The rapid establishment of an ad hoc tribunal for former Yugoslavia might prove to be a testing ground for a permanent international court to try such offences.

221. Although the UN has agreed to the establishment of a tribunal and the Secretary-General is working out the details of its operation with the intention that it should start work soon, there are legal and practical obstacles to its success. A survey of the principal legal difficulties is contained in the memorandum submitted by Professor Peter Rowe.[4] The nature of the conflict, partaking of both civil war and international conflict, with groups of irregular soldiers not under any central command, causes difficulties. "War crimes" have previously been held to occur only in conflicts *between* states, and there is little direct precedent for the framing of charges of "crimes against humanity" by one national of a state against another. There could be difficulties in prosecuting military and political leaders for alleged crimes committed by subordinates where no clear chain of command can be proved. Despite these and other problems, Professor Rowe was sanguine that there would be little difficulty in framing charges under the Genocide Convention of 1948.

222. In addition to these legal difficulties, there are practical considerations. After the Second World War, the victorious powers who established the International Military Tribunal were in a position to execute the sentences passed on those convicted, who were nationals of a defeated enemy power. At present, it does not appear that such "victors' justice" will be available in the case of former Yugoslavia (or indeed Iraq). If any state of whom an alleged criminal was a national refused to hand him over to the tribunal, the Security Council would be faced with three options: to back down, to try the accused *in absentia*[5] or to enforce its demands by further Security Council resolutions involving the usual range of measures up to and including military action. (Security Council Resolution 808 determines that the violations of humanitarian law in former Yugoslavia are a threat to international peace and security, so presumably all necessary means could be used to enforce the work of the tribunal.)

223. The first option would obviously damage the Organisation's credibility, the second would convict but not punish the criminals (thereby also damaging the Organisation) and the third could be enormously controversial. **If the UN's Member States—especially the permanent members of the Security Council—are committed, in the words of the 1945 London Agreement, to the "just and prompt trial and punishment"[6] of war criminals, they must recognise the consequences: these will include making plans for the apprehension and detention of individuals, very possibly in some cases against the wishes of the states where they are resident.**

THE ORGANISATION OF UNITED NATIONS MILITARY OPERATIONS

224. The developing agenda of the United Nations has called into question the way in which UN military operations are organised. Some UN-authorised actions in recent years have marked a departure from what had become accepted UN practice. For instance, neither Operation Desert Storm in Iraq nor Operation Restore Hope in Somalia was carried out under the direct command and control of the Secretary-General, although the UN had a greater degree of involvement in Operation Restore Hope than in Operation Desert Storm. Debate has focused on ways in which the UN, if it is to rely more on the military strength of its Member States, can employ that strength most effectively, while at the same time ensuring that military action is carried out with the full authority of the UN. Witnesses generally agreed that the UN needed to develop a much more effective military capacity, but were divided as to how this could best be achieved.

---

[1] Ev.p 121.
[2] Official Report, 26 April 1993 c 289W.
[3] Q 189.
[4] Ev.pp 327ff.
[5] For a discussion of such trials see Ev.p 332.
[6] Quoted in Ev.p 327.

225. In *An Agenda for Peace*, the Secretary-General argues that until now the Security Council has been unable to operate according to the procedure set out in the Charter when using military force. Article 43 provides for Member States to make available to the UN armed forces for enforcement action to be taken under Chapter VII; the Secretary-General believes that the circumstances now exist for these forces to be put on a permanent footing (para 43). They would be designed to deter or respond to outright aggression, and while not perhaps being capable of dealing with a major army, could deal with military forces "of a lower order". (The Secretary-General makes no recommendation as to forces capable of dealing with major armies). It was not made clear in *An Agenda for Peace* whether these forces were intended to form a standing UN army or to be "earmarked" within the armed forces of Member States. It now seems that the Secretary-General intends these forces to be "earmarked" by Member States rather than forming a standing army.[1]

226. In addition, the Secretary-General proposes the creation of "peace enforcement units". The United Nations has sometimes been called upon to send forces to restore and maintain ceasefires which have been agreed to but not complied with. This task can on occasions exceed the mission of peace-keeping forces and the expectations of governments contributing peace-keeping troops. He suggests that peace enforcement units from Member States could be available on call and would consist of volunteers. They would have to be more heavily armed than peace-keeping forces and would need to undergo extensive preparatory training within their national forces. They would be under the command of the Secretary-General.

227. These proposals received a mixed response from witnesses. The **earmarking of forces** was welcomed by the United Nations Association and Professor Higgins, among others.[2] Sir James Eberle agreed that earmarking by Member States would be more efficient and cost-effective than creating a standing UN force.[3] The Ministry of Defence believed that a standing force would not be practical and would not come about.[4] MoD witnesses stressed that there were no troops within the UK services specifically dedicated to UN activities.[5] They were doubtful of the effectiveness of earmarking specific troops within Member States' forces:

> "We do not regard earmarking as efficient, for the very simple reason that if each nation earmarks troops and declares them to the United Nations, the aggregate of all those declarations is likely to be a rather shapeless force in a military sense."[6]

If peace-keeping troops are to receive special training, it may also make earmarking of troops more difficult.

228. Instead MoD witnesses took the view that it would be more logical for Member States to make a general declaration to the UN that most of their armed forces were available for UN operations. This was the approach adopted in the UK's response to the previous Secretary-General's questionnaire on this subject.[7] It would then be "quite easy" for the United Nations to mix and match the kind of force it needed to establish for a particular operation.[8] According to FCO officials, the UN now preferred to conduct negotiations on troop contributions bilaterally with Member States and the Secretary-General had now "moved away" from the concept of earmarking troops.[9]

229. As well as the practical arguments advanced against the proposal for "earmarked" or standing UN forces there are political ones. Professor Roberts argued that *An Agenda for Peace* failed to take into account the natural disinclination of states to put their troops into the hands of an international body which might employ them for purposes which were "distant from home, or controversial there". They would prefer a system in which troops were made available on an *ad hoc* basis as the need arose, giving them more control over events. This might not in itself be unwelcome, as "the UN itself, even the Security Council, is far from infallible in principle" and some limitations on its powers may not be a bad thing".[10] **Much depends**

---

[1] eg. in *The World Today*, April 1993, p 69.
[2] Ev.p 270,178.
[3] Ev.p 280.
[4] QQ 480–81.
[5] Q 451.
[6] Q 483.
[7] Ev.p 57.
[8] Q 483.
[9] Q 484, Ev.p 57.
[10] Ev.p 309.

on what is meant by "earmarking" forces. If it means that the Secretary-General has first call on particular units within the forces of Member States, we accept its impracticability. If it means that Member States should always use their best endeavours to respond to the Secretary-General's request for troops, as the UK has indicated it would,[1] then we believe this is the right approach.

230. **Peace enforcement units** were regarded by Dr Taylor as "a very good idea" and welcomed by the United Nations Association.[2] Sir John Thomson supported this "extension of the peace-keeping idea" which involved UN forces fighting "in an impartial way", although he accepted that it would be an extremely difficult task for the local commander to carry out.[3] Others were less enthusiastic. The FCO told us that there was "little or no support for such units among Security Council members or other Member States".[4] The Secretary-General's proposal appears to envisage a gradated escalation from peace-keeping (traditionally with the consent of parties) to peace **enforcement**, presumably against the wishes of at least some of the parties. Professor Higgins argued "that the different rôles of peace-keeping and peace enforcement should be appreciated ... if enforcement is needed there is definitionally no concurrent rôle for peace-keeping".[5] She stated that she found the concept of peace enforcement units difficult to understand.[6] The Religious Society of Friends had misgivings about creating such "heavily-armed units".[7] **We do not believe that the Secretary-General's proposal for peace enforcement units is viable. It is difficult to imagine that states will be prepared, or be able to afford, to create special units with the required training and equipment to fight against possibly well armed opponents in a range of possible locations, climates and terrain, that governments will be prepared to accept the possibility of heavy casualties, and that governments will be willing to have these units constantly available for possible duty with the United Nations. Equally it is unlikely that the disputing parties will be prepared to play host to units that might be deployed against their armed forces.**

231. Some of the Secretary-General's recommendations would entail the activation of the **Military Staff Committee** (MSC) of the Security Council.[8] This body, established under Article 47 of the Charter, was designed to "advise and assist the Security Council" on military matters, notably the employment and command of forces placed at its disposal under Article 43. It consists of the chiefs of staff of the five permanent members of the Council, augmented on an *ad hoc* basis by those of other Member States. However, the Committee has never transacted any substantive business and its meetings have been purely formal,[9] although during the Gulf War SCR 665 requested states to use as appropriate mechanisms of the MSC in coordinating actions by naval vessels to ensure compliance with sanctions against Iraq. The Secretary-General makes it clear that the MSC should be involved only in the context of enforcement action under Chapter VII, not in peace-keeping.

232. There was a wide range of opinion concerning the MSC and what its rôle might be. Sir Crispin Tickell thought reviving the MSC was "desirable" as a form of coordinating mechanism in the context of enforcement measures rather than actually running operations.[10] Sir John Thomson was wary of activating the MSC as he believed it would tend to gain power at the expense of the Secretary-General. Peace-keeping had worked fairly well to date and would not be improved by being constantly overseen by the MSC. However, he thought the MSC could concern itself with training, assessing the potential contributions of troops from Member States, etc. Furthermore, the non-permanent members of the Security Council such as Germany and Japan could be coopted onto it.[11] Brigadier Harbottle suggested that the MSC should be designated as an "advisory planning group" for peace-keeping operations.[12] Lord Owen thought that the MSC could have a rôle in providing the Secretary-General with information and expertise on the conduct of modern warfare, ideally working in conjunction with

---

[1] UK Government response to UN Questionnaire on requirements for UN peace-keeping operations.
[2] Ev.p 188,271.
[3] QQ 368,376.
[4] Ev.p 57.
[5] Ev.p 178.
[6] Ev.p 179.
[7] Ev.p 256.
[8] *An Agenda for Peace*, para 43.
[9] Q 30.
[10] Q 374–75.
[11] Q 375.
[12] Ev.p 255–256.

regional agencies such as NATO. Such a planning facility was essential for running UN operations such as that in the former Yugoslavia.[1]

233. MoD and FCO officials regarded the activation of the MSC as a "worst buy" rather than a "best buy".[2] They argued that the MSC had been devised at a time when it was thought the United Nations might develop standing forces of its own; in that context the idea made some sense, but such forces were in their opinion not going to be established. Not only was the idea impractical; it was possible that other Member States would not like the idea of the five permanent members of the United Nations using their military advisers as "a kind of military directorate for the United Nations as a whole".[3] Professor Adam Roberts concluded that this "disparate international committee" was unlikely to be used as the commanding body for large scale military actions for the foreseeable future.[4]

Increasing military advice

234. The Secretary-General has said that "the strength and capability of military staff serving in the Secretariat should be augmented to meet new and heavier requirements".[5] Most witnesses agreed that the Secretary-General needed a better level of military advice and analysis to enable him to operate the expanded range of UN military activity. Some believed that the Military Staff Committee could be adapted to provide this kind of information and expertise. However, the MoD argued in favour of building up the military advice directly available to the Secretary-General.[6]

235. To this end, Ministry of Defence witnesses suggested the creation of a new body for providing military advice to the Secretary-General. This would be:

> "a military policy and planning cell manned by seconded Service officers from the nations, with a number of functions—preparing advice for the Secretary-General on all kinds of operations, all aspects of United Nations operations, developing contingency plans, assessing national capabilities, making proposals for force requirements, command and control, logistics, rules of engagement, training needs, liaising with nations and regional bodies, 24-hour support for current operations and so on and so forth; the kind of military rôle analogous to the sort of thing which goes on in national ministries of defence."[7]

236. Sir James Eberle proposed a similar military planning cell or International Military Support Staff (IMSS). This would not be an operational military headquarters but would provide a senior military element in New York to whom UN field commanders were responsible. The IMSS would carry out a range of tasks in support of UN operations, including: military advice to the Secretary-General, Security Council and commanders in the field; coordination of information from national military sources; preparation of contingency plans for UN deployments; and advice on training to Member States. Sir James pointed out that the location of the IMSS within the UN was a sensitive political matter: it could be part of the staff of the Security Council, or of the Under-Secretary General for Political Affairs. However, he believed that there was a *prima facie* case for it to serve the Military Staff Committee, enlarged (as it could be under the Charter) to include all 15 members of the Security Council.[8] We endorse this proposal (see paragraph 242 below).

237. A need has been expressed by some commentators (most vividly by Major-General Lewis Mackenzie, formerly Commander, UNPROFOR Sarajevo) for there to be a 24-hour presence in UN headquarters in New York, which could respond with advice and if necessary authorization to requests from operational commanders. We were glad to learn from the FCO that there is now a situations room at UN headquarters which is permanently staffed.[9] Such a facility could be expanded to deal with military operations as well as preventive diplomacy. It could also help meet a need expressed to us by military personnel whom we met during our vis-

[1] Q 183.
[2] Q 480.
[3] Q 480.
[4] Ev. p 310.
[5] *An Agenda for Peace*, para 52.
[6] Q 480; details of the current organisation of the military advisers are given in Q 469.
[7] Q 471.
[8] Ev.pp 165–66.
[9] Ev.p 360.

its. They wanted a dedicated liaison officer, with military experience, to be based in New York, responsible for each peace-keeping operation. These posts could be filled on secondment from Member States' armed forces. **We recommend that the Government encourage the augmentation of the new situation room at UN headquarters and the appointment of a liaison officer in New York for each peace-keeping or other military UN operation.**

Devolving military operations

238. However well advised the Secretary-General is, and however effective lines of control and communication are made, it is unlikely that the UN itself will be able to carry out very large scale military operations. The Secretary-General implicitly acknowledges this in *An Agenda for Peace:* he concedes that even the permanent forces he proposes would not be capable of dealing with threats from "a major army equipped with sophisticated weapons".[1] (This description would of course apply to Iraq.) The devolving of military operations to individual Member States or coalitions of Member States (the "hired gun approach to international peacemaking")[2] has been advanced as a way of ameliorating this problem in carrying out larger-scale military operations. Prominent recent examples of this include Operation Desert Storm in Iraq and Operation Restore Hope in Somalia, both led by the USA. The MoD told us that an enforcement operation such as Desert Storm was too big for the United Nations to have handled alone; such large scale operations might be "too difficult for the United Nations to handle or control directly" and that it was unlikely that the UN would obtain the capacity to do so.[3] Baroness Chalker argued that "in some complicated situations" such as Somalia, it was very important to have a unified force.[4] Professor Roberts noted that "experience does seem to show that mobilizing for collective security only works when one power takes the lead".[5] However, it might not be suitable for all forms of UN military action; Dr Prins did not believe that it would be a "satisfactory general solution" for peace-keeping operations, for instance.[6]

239. The circle to be squared is that of giving the UN the muscle to deal with large-scale aggression while ensuring that it is not overloaded to the point of weakening effective command and control. Lord Owen pointed out that one result of greater dependency on regional arrangements by the UN for peace-keeping operations was a change in command structures away from control by the UN. "Inevitably slowly the relationship changes ... where you also had total UN control in New York, now you are bound to have the region having a larger say in the structure".[7] The principal danger of "contracting out" military operations to Member States, coalition or regional organisations is that such military operations will be carried out selectively, when they are in the interests of the states concerned. It has been argued that there is a danger of the US being perceived as the driving force behind the UN's actions—"the UN issues the warrants and the US makes the arrests".[8] The poorer states may see the UN as "the United States and its proximate allies in thin disguise".[9] Greater reliance by the UN on the firepower of the US without adequate Security Council involvement could increase this; and equally, repeated attacks on US (or other great power) intervention could lead to them refusing to take part in future operations. It would be difficult, if not impossible, for the UN to mount certain operations without the logistical support of such powers.

240. Some witnesses were concerned that the credibility of the UN might be seen to depend on the organisation having at its disposal the kind of heavily armed units described in *Agenda for Peace.*[10] **Too much dependence on military force may undermine the UN's valuable rôle as an impartial mediator, especially if such military action is seen as being too much influenced by particular Member States.**

---

[1] Para 43.
[2] Eighth Report of the Committee on External Affairs and Trade, Canadian House of Commons, Ottawa, February 1993.
[3] Q 481.
[4] Q 342.
[5] Ev.p 319.
[6] Ev.p 250.
[7] Q 183.
[8] Eighth Report of the Committee on External Affairs and Trade, Canadian House of Commons, February 1993.
[9] Ev.p 249.
[10] Ev.p 256.

Military operations: the future

241. It is clear that improvements are needed in the way the UN plans for and handles military operations. **There is a need for the UN to think operationally**, as one UN commander in the field told committee members. Equally it is important for the UN not to lose its impartiality and universality and thus its crucial rôle as a trusted mediator in world affairs. Many witnesses have argued in favour of reviving the MSC or creating some new organ to undertake large-scale operations, or sub-contracting the task on a more formal basis to Member States or coalitions thereof. Any consideration of reorganising the military operations of the Organisation should bear in mind the difficulties of attempting anything which involves Charter revision, as our predecessor Committee concluded in 1991.[1]

242. **One way forward for improving the UN's military response would be to bring together the political and the operational command of military actions by means of a committee of the representatives of Security Council members, together with those states contributing to military operations, which would work with and be advised by a permanent military planning cell. The cell could develop contingency plans for operations and provide 24-hour support for current operations in the ways suggested by the Ministry of Defence and Sir James Eberle, but it would report to the Secretary-General.**

243. Such a structure might make the control of such actions more operationally effective. Furthermore, it would allow the "new" world powers such as Japan and Germany, which are likely to contribute financially and militarily more to UN operations, to have a greater say. Thus the command of the UN, especially of its military actions, would be seen as being more representative of the organisation without revision of the Charter being necessary. Lord Gladwyn suggested a similar approach—a temporary enlargement of the Military Staff Committee and changes in its operation.[2]

244. In addition, **UN commanders in the field need to be chosen with care on the basis of merit**—there have been some cases in the past of UN operations suffering due to the low calibre of their chiefs.[3] Once a high-quality commander is in place, there is a need for him to be given greater responsibility—the military commanders of large operations such as UNOSOM II in Somalia should not have to refer operational decisions back to New York for approval. (CARE, for instance, believed that the commander of UNOSOM in Somalia needed authority to exercise his own military discretion[4]). This is one aspect of a general concern that the best way forward for more effective UN operations, both military and civilian, is greater devolving of responsibility down the management structure into the field. Changes of this kind would make it easier for the Secretary-General to get positive answers to his requests for troops, as Member States would have more confidence that their forces will be deployed in professionally-run operations. One reason why military commanders prefer working within either a national force or a long-standing multinational organisation (such as NATO) is that they are more involved in the selection of the composition and size of forces at their disposal for any particular operation. **It would undoubtedly help the Secretary-General to collect forces from Member States if it was clear that the force commander appointed for an operation was given some say in the make-up of the troops at his disposal. Such decisions should not be transferred entirely from the Secretary-General's responsibility, as this would be seen to detract from the impartial nature of the UN's operations. What is required is a high level input by force commanders before deployment.**

Training

245. During our visits to former Yugoslavia, Somalia and Cambodia we were struck by the high standard of understanding the UN troops showed of the political as well as the military context in which they were working. As MoD witnesses told us, UN soldiers face much more demanding and varied tasks than they used to, and therefore "there is a need for even greater professionalism" than exists at the moment.[5] New structures for command and control of UN military operations will clearly have to be accompanied by the highest possible level of training

---

[1] The Middle East after the Gulf War, Third Report from the Foreign Affairs Committee, HC143 (1990–91) para 7.10.
[2] Ev.p 326.
[3] Cf Brian Urquhart, *A Life in Peace and War*, 1987, p 148, for an example
[4] Ev.p 28.
[5] Q 475.

of the troops who will have to go on undertaking the difficult, dangerous and sometimes almost impossible duties placed on them by the international community.

246. The Secretary-General recommends that "arrangements be reviewed and improved for training peace-keeping personnel".[1] This proposal has generally been welcomed by governments of Member States. For instance President Bush proposed that the US should offer facilities for the joint training of peace-keeping troops of different Member States.[2] Mr Hogg told us that he hoped UK troops could train alongside troops from countries with "even greater expertise" in peace-keeping, such as Canada and the Nordic States.[3] Professor Higgins also supported common training for peace-keeping.[4] The United Nations Association drew our attention to the multinational training exercises carried out by the Nordic countries, and suggested that peace-keeping courses should be "an integral part of every soldier's training".[5] Sir James Eberle recommended the establishment of a "UN Defence College" on the model of the NATO Defence College, as the success of NATO has resulted in part from the training received at the NATO Defence College.[6]

247. Ministry of Defence officials told us that a variety of training programmes was used depending on the particular operation to be undertaken. For instance, the Cheshire regiment were trained "over a long period"—five weeks—before deployment in Bosnia. Training for UN operations was featuring more in the syllabus of staff college courses as awareness of, and participation in, UN operations increased.[7]

248. Members of the Committee were concerned to hear, during their visit to Cambodia, that some of the soldiers there did not feel that their services in such missions would be properly appreciated and seen as good for their career development. Ministry of Defence officials told us that servicemen and women were assessed on how well they did each job, not on the particular job done; furthermore, the standard posting to a UN position was only six months.[8] However, **if the UK (and other Member States) wish to continue to provide motivated high-quality volunteers for UN operations, these service personnel must be convinced that their service will be recognised as an important part of their military careers.**

249. The Ministry of Defence also told us that a comprehensive feedback mechanism operated to ensure that experience of UN work was returned into the forces' collective memory.[9] This is obviously an important point, touched on by other witnesses and one which could apply to civilian as well as to military aspects of UN operations.[10] Without effective feedback of this sort, there could be a danger of "re-inventing the wheel" on each occasion that UK troops are involved in UN operations. During our visit to Cambodia, it was suggested to us that an independent historian be attached to each UN operation to produce an official history of it. **We recommend that a formal system of reporting back on each UN operation be developed, on which governments contributing military or civilian personnel to UN operations can draw, so that the lessons learned from each UN operation are heeded in future operations.**

VIII IMPLICATIONS FOR UNITED KINGDOM POLICY

250. Britain's **special rôle** as a Permanent Member of the Security Council means that the expansion of UN activities and their changing nature has a more significant impact on the UK than on many other states. Britain's long-standing diplomatic experience, its active participation in major international institutions such as NATO and its effective military capability give further weight to this rôle. The changing nature of the work of the United Nations since 1987 and widening definitions of what constitutes international intervention have had a number of significant effects and the implications for government policy flowing from them are substantial.

---

[1] *An Agenda for Peace*, para 52.
[2] Ev.pp 249,271.
[3] Q 155; Ev.p 3.
[4] Q 417.
[5] Ev.p 271.
[6] Ev.p 280–281.
[7] Q 459.
[8] Q 514.
[9] QQ 459,513–14.
[10] eg. the United Nations Association Ev.p 271.

251. There has been a marked increase in meetings of the Security Council, and in Security Council resolutions (72 in 1992). Permanent members of the Council have as a result to lobby more intensively to achieve the resolutions they want and then have to devote diplomatic resources to ensuring they are put into effect. The Permanent Under-Secretary of State at the FCO gave us a graphic account of the work involved in achieving this.[1] Member States are sending their diplomats and other civil servants to assist in UN operations (e.g. in the former Yugoslavia). There has been a general increase in the workload of the FCO, both in posts (not just the UK missions in New York and Geneva) and a consequent rearrangement of departments within the FCO.[2] The increasing pressure of UN affairs had meant that there are fewer staff to attend to other aspects of UK foreign policy. We were told that the work of the UN, in particular the continuing work arising from UNCED and Agenda 21, had increased the ODA's workload, resulting in some departments increasing their staff.[3]

252. Other aspects of the UN's developments put extra burdens on the Foreign and Commonwealth Office. Developments in international law as the definition of "threats to international peace and security" is being extended and plans to put into practice the UN's decision to establish an *ad hoc* UN-sponsored war crimes tribunal all increase the workload of diplomatic and legal sections of the FCO. The coordination between the UN and regional organisations (EC, NATO, WEU and CSCE in Yugoslavia) and the necessary development of the rôle and aims of such organisations also requires an increased diplomatic effort. The UK is also firmly committed to management, budgetary and other reform designed to improve the performance of the UN, which represent another burden on the Diplomatic Service. There are also effects on other government departments, including the deployment of Customs and Excise staff to Sanctions Assistance Missions in former Yugoslavia. Increased UN activity is putting huge strains on the United Kingdom's diplomatic staffing: the Foreign Secretary told us on 16 June 1993 that staff were being taken from elsewhere to cope with the extra workload.[4] **The Government should recognise the staffing implications for the diplomatic service of the expanding workload of the United Nations.**

253. The Secretary-General has asked that governments of Members States do all they can to increase the information available to the Secretariat for the purposes of fact-finding, preventive diplomacy and enforcement. There are obvious uses for fact-finding and preventive diplomacy—the Secretary-General needs to be as well-informed as possible about the potential for conflict, natural or man-made disaster and violation of human rights if he is to carry out his tasks of "good offices", and of warning the Security Council about these dangers. This could include military intelligence, e.g. the results of satellite reconnaissance.

254. In addition to this need for information, there is the information required for peace-making and enforcement. Examples of this include the information given by the UK to the UN Special Commission on Iraq about British firms involved in arms trading with Iraq and to the IAEA on potential violations of the Nuclear Non-Proliferation Treaty (although such action at an earlier stage might have reduced the massive increase in Iraq's military power). The work of British Customs and Excise has involved giving information about possible breaches of the Yugoslav sanctions regime by British companies.

255. **Given the increasing range of complexity of the UN's activities, and the importance placed on the need for the Secretariat to be as well informed as possible, there can only be an expansion in the amount of information which is expected to be given to the UN Secretariat by Member States, in particular by the UK and other permanent members of the Security Council.**

256. **The number of British troops committed to UN peace-keeping has increased from 800 to 3,700 in the last two years.[5] UN peace-keeping operations (to which permanent members of the Security Council are contributing more and more, after many years of a self-denying ordinance) are likely to continue and will represent a continuing charge on the resources of Member States.** In addition, the use of Member States' armed forces to enforce UN resolutions, as in the case of Operation Desert Storm or in activities based upon Security Council Resolutions enforcing the no-fly zones in northern and southern Iraq, obviously costs more than the traditional UN

---

[1] Minutes of Evidence 17 March 1993, Q 18, HC 562, 1992–93
[2] Ev.pp 315–320.
[3] Ev.p 150–52.
[4] Minutes of Evidence of the Foreign Affairs Committee, 16 June 1993, HC 752, 1992–93, Q 52.
[5] Q 455.

peace-keeping operations, which involved fewer less heavily-armed troops. **Any increase in military enforcement of UN resolutions will proportionately increase the costs, and MoD witnesses admitted that enforcement activity would be an even more severe challenge in terms of organisation than peace-keeping.**[1] **Similarly the use of military protection for humanitarian operations may well increase and could have serious financial, logistical and manpower implications for the United Kingdom.**

257. Finally, if the UK is keen to increase the military support given to the UN Secretariat, there will obviously be more secondments of senior UK military personnel to the UN, adding another pressure to the already stretched services. (We expect that the Defence Committee will comment on the relationship between all these new tasks and the 'Options for Change' review in its report on UK Peace-keeping and Intervention Forces.)

258. Although the regular budget of the UN has remained constant in real terms in the last few years (and the pressure for achieving this stability has been partly due to the UK) the costs of UN peace-keeping have risen dramatically. As a significant contributor to the UN's costs, the UK has automatically been paying more in UN dues as a result. Voluntary contributions to the UN have also increased, such as the UK contribution to the cost of UN guards in Iraq and the government's contribution to the UN's electoral fund. Likewise the ODA has been paying more towards the cost of UN humanitarian operations as these have become ever more complex and expensive.[2] Finally, there is an inherent cost in enforcing sanctions, comprising possible loss of trade, any costs arising from compensation to countries disadvantaged by complying with a sanctions regime, and assistance given to countries to ensure compliance (e.g the SAMs in countries in and bordering the former Yugoslavia). **The financial implications of the expansion of the UN's rôle all raise serious issues vis a vis the UK's spending priorities which will have to be addressed.**

259. Information programmes on the aims, activities and operations of the UN help ordinary people to identify with the work and objectives of the organisation. **The UK Government should therefore try to ensure greater understanding and support for the work of the United Nations in schools, colleges and universities.**

260. The formidable list of consequences for the UK of the expansion of the UN's work, and the UK's continuing commitment to strengthen the rôle of the United Nations in the prevention and resolution of conflicts[3] mean that the UK will have to maintain a sufficient diplomatic staff of high calibre to ensure that it can undertake the tasks set out above. It will need to ensure that any changes to the rôle, composition or procedures of the Security Council manage to balance the natural demands of equity with the vital importance of maintaining its effectiveness. It must ensure that the Secretary-General has adequate military advice from within his office, and, where appropriate, from some kind of military planning cell or a revamped Military Staff Committee composed of staff from Member States, so that he can properly run the new generation of UN peace-keeping (and peace enforcement) operations. It will need to continue its efforts with other Member States to improve the efficiency and effectiveness of the Secretariat and the specialised agencies; as the range of the UN's activities increases, it will be more important than ever to ensure that costs are kept within reasonable bounds and value is obtained for money spent. Money can be saved by an increased use of preventive diplomacy rather than peace-keeping, and the UK should ensure that the Secretary-General is given as much assistance as possible to enable him to carry out this vital function. **All in all, the Government's commitment to furthering the work of the UN will require a commitment to creating a Foreign and Commonwealth Office for the twenty-first century which is equipped to undertake that necessary work.**

IX CONCLUSIONS

261. Since the disintegration of the Cold War balance of power, demands for the United Nations to try to resolve conflict, or to relieve suffering or abuse, have dramatically increased. The United Nations' response has been to extend the number, type and scale of its operations. The outstanding success of the UN-authorised operation led by the USA to reverse Iraq's act

[1] Q 475–77.
[2] See Cm 2202, pp 31,40.
[3] *Ibid* p 13.

of aggression against Kuwait and the successful operation in Namibia have been followed by new demands for the UN to take action in situations far more complex than the act of invasion by one country of a neighbouring state. In Cambodia about 16,000 troops wearing blue berets have been deployed together with very large numbers of civilian personnel; in Somalia the number is around 28,000. Over thirty countries have contributed personnel to each of those operations. The operation in former Yugoslavia has been extended from the original peace-keeping operation in Croatia and a narrowly defined humanitarian relief operation in Bosnia. It is conceivable that UN personnel will be deployed there in even greater numbers than in Cambodia or Somalia. In both Somalia and Bosnia humanitarian relief operations are becoming enforcement operations carried out by heavily armed international troops backed up by air power. It seems possible that the UN will be called upon to maintain its presence for a long time in both countries. At the same time as these massive interventions, there are ten other UN peace-keeping operations at the time we complete this Report, of which one, in Mozambique, is planned to involve 8,000 troops.

262. Hope for a better international order lies in the growing acceptance by states, governments and even potentially warring factions within states that conflicts of the kind we have described should be resolved by political negotiation and not by military force. That acceptance will be achieved more quickly if UN preventive diplomacy is made more credible and effective. Such credibility could be enhanced by the growing deterrent value of the United Nations Security Council's powers and their increasing application—the threat of sanctions and blockades and the possibility of direct military action.

263. The United Nations was not established to be the world's ubiquitous policeman. Its uneven record of success to date in dealing with the new and increasing demands being placed upon it confirms our view that expectations about what it can achieve have been raised too high. The United Nations cannot wipe away the tear in every eye, compel people everywhere to live peacefully with their neighbours, or stop fighting where there is no will to stop. It would be wrong, however, to condemn the United Nations or to judge the future effectiveness of Security Council powers on the basis of the extreme situation it is attempting to tackle in Bosnia. We cannot over emphasise the seismic change that has occurred in UN Security Council activity. It is so easy to criticize and condemn the fact that the UN has fallen short of expectations during this crucial new phase in its development. But the demands have placed a near-impossible strain upon a UN security system whose new rôles are only five or six years old. There are circumstances where it can try to help, persuade or pressurize governments, and groups within states, not to resort to force or to end conflicts, or can encourage, and help to ensure respect for, internationally agreed fundamental human rights and democratic decision-making structures within states. There is a wide range of ways in which it can intervene. These range from diplomatic, behind-the-scenes persuasion, through deployment of personnel, including soldiers, to monitor, warn against and discourage acts of aggression or in support of other UN agencies to try to save lives, to the outright use of military force. New techniques are evolving as a result of experience in the field. Some of the proposals in *An Agenda for Peace* have already been implemented in a piecemeal fashion. Our Report describes a range of practical ways in which the work of the United Nations could be made more effective, which we call upon the United Kingdom Government to support—especially ways of extending the diplomatic and other preventive work of the Organisation, its Secretary-General and the other UN agencies.

264. The most intractable issue is this: when should there be military intervention? How and when should the world community, acting together in the United Nations, go beyond persuasion and decide to cross the Rubicon into actual military involvement? Should it try to do so in every conflict or humanitarian disaster where the Secretary-General and the Security Council conclude that there is a threat to international peace and security? Or only as a last resort? And if so, what scope is left for the impartiality of humanitarian assistance or the concept (described by Brian Urquhart) of 'non-violent' army activity at the international level—which of course is the traditional and idealist view of the rôle of UN troops.

265. Plainly, as we have said, it is not practicable for the UN to attempt everything. But how is the selection to be made? Events in Bosnia and Somalia provide examples of the way in which one kind of intervention can slide and swell into another, with the original mission to save lives and protect relief workers becoming transformed into a major military undertaking,

and with UN 'peace-keeping' troops being driven into enforcement actions which may mean taking sides and even having to use force against the people they are supposed to be assisting.

266. Such unpredictability about the way events take hold adds even greater uncertainty and risk to the process of deciding whether to intervene. Crucial issues of sovereignty and the rights of minorities to self-determination have to be confronted. Each crisis, and each case, raises different and novel aspects which make intervention 'by the rules' harder to implement. We nevertheless believe that some clearer criteria for UN action in these new conditions, some codification of principles, can and must be formulated if the UN's authority and effectiveness are to be upheld and enhanced.

267. **We suggest that proposals for the UN to become involved in an area of conflict, in however limited a manner initially, should be tested by the Security Council against the following key considerations:**

   — **First, has the UN a locus? Is there a rôle for it in the conflict in question or in its potential consequences; and can that rôle be effectively played by means short of military force?**

   — **Second, are the objectives of the proposed military intervention realistic and likely to be obtained?**

   — **Third, given the likelihood of escalation into more and more intervention of a political and a military kind (however modest the initial intervention), is the Security Council prepared to recognise the full consequences of a prolonged and extensive operation? Have the members the political will and the determination to see matters through to a conclusion?**

   — **Finally, and most crucially, if the Security Council is so committed, are Member States prepared to mobilise the resources, manpower, cash and equipment and to match their words with deeds for however long it takes to complete the operation?**

268. We see this as the key. **Only if UN members, accepting the leadership of the Security Council, are prepared to stick with the intervention all the way, and to be ready to provide the necessary resources, the personnel and the finance, does it make sense to embark upon an undertaking in the first place. And only the knowledge that this degree of commitment to the possible use of force is there makes it possible for UN diplomacy to carry credibility at the earlier and preventive stages.**

269. There is finally the question of the UN's capacity to implement actions once decided upon and to sustain the full trust and endorsement of its membership as events unfold and tasks expand. Our Report has examined in detail some of the logistical, financial, military and organisational challenges facing the UN today. Our detailed conclusions and recommendations are set out below.

270. **As a long-standing permanent member of the Security Council, the British Government must ensure that its own structures and policies are adapted to the increasingly heavy responsibilities involved. A Foreign and Commonwealth Office fully equipped to fulfil this rôle, and to meet the new burdens which it places on active and leading members of the United Nations, is certainly one of the basic requirements in this context.**

LIST OF RECOMMENDATIONS AND CONCLUSIONS

Preventive diplomacy

1.   We agree with the Secretary-General that a UN fact-finding mission can help to defuse a dispute by its presence, indicating to the parties that the Organisation, and in particular the Security Council, is actively seized of the matter as a present or potential threat to international security. (Para 43)

2.   We agree that the Secretary-General should have access to the best possible information to enable him to do his job. We recommend that the UK Government discuss with the Secretary-General and the other permanent members of the Security Council the feasibility of providing him with information held by national intelligence agencies so that the UN is better aware of potential threats to international peace and security. (Para 50)

3.   We recommend that the UK Government exert pressure for the UN Secretariat to be reorganised. We believe staff should be deployed from other, less vital, areas of the UN Secretariat, to increase the capacity of the Department of Political Affairs in preventive diplomacy. (Para 51)

4.   Preventive diplomacy, even backed up by more effective mechanisms for the provision of information and analysis to the Secretary-General should not be seen as a panacea. Even were the Secretariat to be fully informed and the Secretary-General to draw the attention of the Security Council to potential crises, the essential elements in any timely and effective United Nations action are the political will to act upon that information, the capacity to execute the decision and favourable responses from the disputants. Preventive diplomacy must also be backed up by a determination by the Security Council to take tougher action if the parties fail to respond. (Para 52)

Preventive deployment and demilitarised zones

5.   We recommend that the UK as a permanent member of the Security Council support the deployment of UN missions in a preventive capacity. (Para 58)

6.   We support the concept of creating demilitarised zones as a preventive mechanism. (Para 59)

7.   We believe that the experiment in Macedonia should be seen as an encouraging precedent for similar deployments in other potential trouble spots. As with the other preventive mechanisms of the UN, we believe that here too the acceptability and success of such operations rests on a clear understanding that behind them lie credible pressures and sanctions that can, if prevention fails, be deployed by the UN. (Para 60)

Peace-keeping

8.   The success of all UN peace-keeping operations has depended crucially on the willingness of Member States to provide the cash and military resources to make them effective. (Para 63)

9.   The nature of the conflicts in which the UN is being called upon to intervene has changed (Para 65)

10.   The Security Council must ensure that peace-keeping operations are not deployed unless there is a reasonable chance of success. It may be necessary for the Council to resist demands, demonstrate that conditions are not propitious and insist that some other method than peace-keeping should be used. (Para 90)

11.   Once UN military forces are present they are liable to be used in a range of ways. Contributing states will always insist that the remit for their forces is laid down in precise terms. But while this might be possible *initially*, once on the ground there will be pressures for their rôle to be extended. (Para 91)

12.   Any successful UN operation must have a practicable mandate and the support of the Security Council; where there is no cooperation from the parties to the conflict, the UN must decide whether it wishes to attempt to impose its solutions on the situation. Peace-keeping is a consent-based, impartial activity; enforcement is not. We believe that there must be a clear distinction between the two activities and that there are grave difficulties in combining them in a given location. (Para 92)

13.   We consider that calls for military deployment on the ground to enforce in Bosnia a disputed peace plan have been misconceived: troops equipped for peace-keeping or humanitarian protection work cannot be transformed into a UN fighting force simply by passing a new Security Council resolution. Security Council Resolution 836 extended the mandate of UNPROFOR to enable it to deter attacks against the safe areas and to begin to implement part of the Vance-Owen plan. We are not persuaded that it is practicable to try to impose a peace plan in Bosnia from outside. We fear that attempting so to impose a plan for the constitutional structure of part of former Yugoslavia could make things worse rather than better for the civilian population as well as having serious consequences for the safety of UN personnel there, which includes a large British contingent, and for the future willingness of governments to allow UN peacekeepers into their states. It may also affect governments' willingness to contribute troops to UN operations in the future. (Para 94)

14.   Experience of recent peace-keeping operations, and in particular the experiences in Bosnia and Cambodia lead us to the conclusion that the Security Council must be persuaded to recognise that not all proposals for peace-keeping operations can be put into effect successfully. We urge the United Kingdom to use its influence in the Security Council to ensure that peace-keeping operations, particularly on the scale of these recent operations, are entered into only when there is a realistic prospect of their objectives being achieved. Where the UN does decide to intervene, we recommend that the mandates laid down for UN military and civilian operations be rigorously scrutinised to try to ensure their practicability and that no commitment to a peace-keeping operation be entered into by the Security Council unless there is a firm prospect of the necessary resources—human and financial—being available from the Member States to allow the operation a realistic chance of being fully implemented. (Para 95)

Humanitarian intervention and assistance

15.   Humanitarian intervention does not always inevitably involve use of the military. Military intervention for humanitarian purposes is a new phenomenon for the United Nations. It has happened to protect aid convoys (as in former Yugoslavia), distribute food directly (as in military air lifts to Sarajevo and other parts of Bosnia and Somalia), to protect areas designated as safe havens or safe areas (as in Iraq and now in Bosnia) and to help to rebuild a civil society (as in Somalia). (Para 98)

16.   The old constraints embodied in Article 2.7 of the Charter against interference in matters which are "essentially" domestic are no longer accepted. The change is a very recent one and has occurred in response to two very different emergencies: in Somalia and in Iraq after the Gulf War. Decisions to intervene militarily on humanitarian grounds have not been taken according to a clear set of guiding principles, but in response to sudden emergencies. The UN has not so intervened in other humanitarian disasters of perhaps comparable scale—such as that in Sudan. Better criteria, which are internationally accepted, need to be drawn up to determine the circumstances in which armed intervention for humanitarian purposes is acceptable. The criteria listed in paragraph 102 above may form a good basis on which to build. In the end, however, the decision on whether actually to intervene militarily for humanitarian purposes will depend on each occasion on the exact circumstances of the emergency in question. (Para 110)

Human rights

17.   The FCO stated that the Government was keen for the UN to play a more prominent rôle in the field of human rights, and sought to improve the implementation of the

existing human rights instruments and to assist states to fulfil their international obligations in this field, as well as supporting increased funding for the human rights organs of the UN. We support these aims. (Para 114)

18. The Government should support the abolition or rationalisation of UN organs that have outlived their usefulness if this is necessary to release resources for the UN's human rights work. (Para 115)

19. We recommend that the Government, given its long-standing commitment to human rights, make a substantial contribution to the UN's human rights Trust Fund. Compatibility should be ensured between the government's actions within the UN and its "good government" decisions. (Para 116)

20. Debate at the World Conference on Human Rights in Vienna in June 1993 demonstrated that maintaining international consensus on definitions of human rights, let alone whether to enforce such rights is not practicable. (Para 118)

21. As with intervention on other humanitarian grounds, decisions on whether to intervene on human rights grounds will always be exceptionally delicate ones for the UN to contemplate and can only be decided on a pragmatic, case by case, basis. Nevertheless, the UN must always be conscious of its responsibility to act and to be seen to be acting in a consistent and even-handed way. (Para 118)

22. The exposure of massive human rights abuses is a proper rôle of the UN and we support the Secretary-General's proposal referred to in paragraph 45 above that such violations be brought to the attention of the Security Council. We recommend that the Government press for the Secretary-General to give regular reports, at least annually, to the Security Council on human rights violation. (Para 119)

Sanctions

23. The EC's sanctions assistance missions in countries neighbouring the former Yugoslavia are a valuable innovation, and we support the Government's commitment of staff to them. (Para 125)

24. Limited sanctions do not seem to us to have proved successful; if the UN wishes to use sanctions as an effective weapon they need to be accompanied from the start by a blockade, by land, sea and air, and by a sophisticated range of controls over commercial, financial and trading mechanisms. (Para 130)

25. While sanctions can never be 100% effective they could be made more effective than they have proved in the past. In general they are effective only if maintained over a long period; so the international community, if it wishes to encourage states to participate fully in implementing them, may have to be prepared, in effect, to pay them to do so. We recommend that the government encourage discussion within the Security Council to develop a mechanism for providing financial help to states affected by sanctions. If Member States are committed to using third countries as a significant tool of enforcement, they will have to be prepared both for the cost they will incur in terms of loss of trade, and to back them up with force if necessary. (Para 131)

Military enforcement

26. It is probable that many of the future disasters of the world will be located in similar situations to that found in Somalia, where civil war, territorial disputes and a disparity between geographic boundaries and ethnic realities may mean that the UN may not be able to negotiate with governments. Equally, it is in just such circumstances that the demand for the UN's help may be most pressing, and where the use of military force to ensure the UN's help is delivered may be needed most and where there may be the greatest unease about the employment of such force. We believe that the amount of force used should be such as not to alienate substantial proportions of a population. Inordinate force can be wholly counterproductive and endanger the activities of non-governmental organisations. (Para 135)

27.   Disagreement between the USA and European powers about whether, and how, to enforce compliance with the Vance-Owen plan for Bosnia has illustrated, at the least, the difficulties of UN-sponsored efforts to impose a settlement and enforce peace from outside. (Para 141)

28.   Mandates for the military enforcement of UN actions should be as clear as the consensus-based nature of UN politics allows. Enforcement action by the UN will only make practical sense if the Member States are willing to provide the military and logistical resources required and if the political will to use those resources exists, recognising that a process of enforcement may take a great many years and lead to large numbers of casualties. (Para 145)

Cooperation with regional arrangements

29.   We endorse the shift in attitude shown in *An Agenda for Peace* and the acceptance that there has to be a partnership between regional organisations and the UN, not a shuffling off of responsibilities between them. (Para 156)

30.   All recommendations for the improvement of the UN's performance must start from the basis that it neither can nor should try to do everything. Its job should be as much to help others to solve problems as to solve them itself. Hence our emphasis on the need for the UN wherever possible to take advantage of the expertise and experience of other players, be they NATO, NGOs or others. But the *authority* of the United Nations in matters of international security is crucial: we agree with witnesses that force should not be employed by regional organisations on behalf of the UN without the explicit authority of the Security Council. (Para 157)

Financing the United Nations

31.   We do not believe that donations from the private sector would have much impact on the UN's financial position; furthermore, it would be inappropriate for an organisation of sovereign states to be significantly dependent on private donations. (Para 167)

32.   We agree with the proposal that payments to the UN's regular budget should be made on a quarterly basis rather than as a annual lump sum, and that under such a system it would be appropriate for interest to be charged on late payments. (Para 168)

33.   A three-year rather than a ten-year average of Member States' national income would provide a much fairer assessment of their ability to pay their contribution to the UN's budget. We recommend that the Government support this proposal in discussion of future UN financing. (Para 169)

34.   We agree that, given the necessity for prompt deployment of peace-keeping operations, the United Nations peace-keeping reserve fund (or "start-up" fund) should be increased from $150 million to $400 million. (Para 172)

35.   We recommend that the Government support proposals to establish an annual peace-keeping assessment, perhaps payable (as we have suggested for the regular budget) on a quarterly basis. (Para 173)

36.   We consider it essential that the FCO is fully compensated through the public expenditure system for any unforeseen demands on its Vote arising out of peace-keeping policy decisions. (Para 175)

37.   The proper funding of the Organisation will depend on Member States demonstrating their commitment to the UN by paying the contributions which are required of them by law. (Para 176)

Institutional change

38.   We do not believe that it is practical to expect the permanent members of the Security Council as presently constituted to give up their right to the veto. (Para187)

39.   Although there are strong arguments for and against enlarging the Security Council we do not consider it likely that the General Assembly would agree to give Japan and Germany permanent membership of the Security Council without giving it to other states; obtaining agreement within the membership on the identity of those states is likely to be extremely difficult. (Para 188)

40.   It is clear that the debate over the composition of the Security Council will continue and the UK must be prepared to take a constructive approach to it (Para 189)

41.   The regular meetings of the so-called "core group"—the permanent five plus states with a particular involvement in financing, or contributing forces to, an opera-tion—are a welcome development. They allow the permanent five members to undertake the fullest consultation with the other key countries in any operation without the effectiveness of the Security Council's decision-making capacity being impaired. This allows Member States who contribute financially and logistically, especially to the UN's ever-increasing military rôle, to have a more powerful voice in the ways in which military force is employed, while avoiding the need for poten-tially divisive changes to the UN Charter. (Para 189)

42.   Whether or not changes are made to the composition of the Security Council the FCO told us that there is no pressure for Britain to give up its permanent member-ship and our impression from visits and the balance of evidence received tends to confirm this. (Para 190)

43.   Given the range of tasks expected of him, the choice of Secretary-General, and the support (logistical and political) he receives are both absolutely crucial. (Para 191)

44.   Consideration should be given to greater delegation by the Secretary-General of some of his tasks, perhaps by the appointment of a deputy Secretary-General to share the burden. (Para 192)

45.   We agree with the view expressed by non-governmental organisations that more devolved responsibility is needed within the UN system, which is "over-centralised and bureaucratic". (Para 198)

46.   We agree with Baroness Chalker that efforts to reform the agencies should be concen-trated on ensuring that there is "more work at the coalface and perhaps less in the boardroom". (Para 198)

47.   The Department of Humanitarian Affairs has not yet been able to fulfil the intentions behind its establishment to improve the UN's coordination of its emergency response. It has been in existence for little more than a year. It is too early to pass judgement on its performance. (Para 204)

48.   We consider that the Secretary-General should be given full support in his effort to develop the concept of interim UN offices where the organisation of all UN per-sonnel in a country can be brought together. (Para 205)

49.   In considering how best to improve the UN's humanitarian response, an *ad hoc* approach is inevitable: every crisis is unique. The key for the UN as far as organi-sational effectiveness is concerned is to find the most appropriate postholder or lead agency and give it overall command. (Para 206)

50.   Effective cooperation between the UN and other humanitarian organisations is as important as that between the UN agencies themselves. (Para 207)

51.   Early warning of potential humanitarian disasters, in which organisations outside the UN have an important part to play, should enable the UN to become involved sooner in situations which also frequently have serious implications for interna-tional peace and security. (Para 210)

52.   Appointments from outside the UN career service might bring fresh thinking into the Organisation and encourage cultural change. We agree with the local representative of a UN agency in Somalia who told members that the UN needed to break some of its traditional conventions and learn new ways of working. We recommend that where appropriate the UN should utilise relevant expertise to do more of the liaison work currently done by full-time UN employees. (Para 223)

An international criminal court

53.   If the UN's Member States—especially the permanent members of the Security Council—are committed, in the words of the 1945 London Agreement, to the "just and prompt trial and punishment" of war criminals, they must recognise the consequences: these will include making plans for the apprehension and detention of individuals, very possibly in some cases against the wishes of the states where they are resident. (Para 223)

Organisation of United Nations military operations

54.   Much depends on what is meant by "earmarking" forces. If it means that the Secretary-General has first call on particular units within the forces of Member States, we accept its impracticability. If it means that Member States should always use their best endeavours to respond to the Secretary-General's request for troops, as the UK has indicated it would, then we believe this is the right approach. (Para 229)

55.   We do not believe that the Secretary-General's proposal for peace enforcement units is viable. It is difficult to imagine that states will be prepared, or be able to afford, to create special units with the required training and equipment to fight against possibly well armed opponents in a range of possible locations, climates and terrain, that governments will be prepared to accept the possibility of heavy casualties, and that governments will be willing to have these units constantly available for possible duty with the United Nations. Equally it is unlikely that the disputing parties will be prepared to play host to units that might be deployed against their armed forces. (Para 230)

56.   We recommend that the Government encourage the augmentation of the new situation room at UN headquarters and the appointment of a liaison officer in New York for each peace-keeping or other military UN operation. (Para 237)

57.   Too much dependence on military force may undermine the UN's valuable rôle as an impartial mediator, especially if such military action is seen as being too much influenced by particular Member States. (Para 240)

58.   There is a need for the UN to think operationally (Para 241)

59.   One way forward for improving the UN's military response would be to bring together the political and the operational command of military actions by means of a committee of the representatives of Security Council members, together with those states contributing to military operations, which would work with and be advised by a permanent military planning cell. The cell could develop contingency plans for operations and provide 24-hour support for current operations in the ways suggested by the Ministry of Defence and Sir James Eberle, but it would report to the Secretary-General. (Para 242)

60.   UN commanders in the field need to be chosen with care on the basis of merit (Para 244)

61.   It would undoubtedly help the Secretary-General to collect forces from Member States if it was clear that the force commander appointed for an operation was given some say in the make-up of the troops at his disposal. Such decisions should not be transferred entirely from the Secretary-General's responsibility, as this would be seen to detract from the impartial nature of the UN's operations. What is required is a high level input by force commanders before deployment. (Para 244)

62.   If the UK (and other Member States) wish to continue to provide motivated high-
       quality volunteers for UN operations, these service personnel must be convinced
       that their service will be recognised as an important part of their military careers.
       (Para 248)

63.   We recommend that a formal system of reporting back on each UN operation be
       developed, on which governments contributing military or civilian personnel to UN
       operations can draw, so that the lessons learned from each UN operation are
       heeded in future operations. (Para 249)

Implications for United Kingdom policy

64.   The Government should recognise the staffing implications for the diplomatic service
       of the expanding workload of the United Nations. (Para 252)

65.   Given the increasing range of complexity of the UN's activities, and the importance
       placed on the need for the Secretariat to be as well informed as possible, there can
       only be an expansion in the amount of information which is expected to be given
       to the UN Secretariat by Member States, in particular by the UK and other per-
       manent members of the Security Council. (Para 255)

66.   The number of British troops committed to UN peace-keeping has increased from 800
       to 3,700 in the last two years. UN peace-keeping operations (to which permanent
       members of the Security Council are contributing more and more, after many years
       of a self-denying ordinance) are likely to continue and will represent a continuing
       charge on the resources of Member States. (Para 256)

67.   Any increase in military enforcement of UN resolutions will proportionately increase
       the costs, and MoD witnesses admitted that enforcement activity would be an even
       more severe challenge in terms of organisation than peace-keeping. Similarly the
       use of military protection for humanitarian operations may well increase and could
       have serious financial, logistical and manpower implications for the United
       Kingdom. (Para 256)

68.   The financial implications of the expansion of the UN's rôle all raise serious issues vis
       a vis the UK's spending priorities which will have to be addressed. (Para 258)

69.   The UK Government should try to ensure greater understanding and support for the
       work of the United Nations in schools, colleges and universities. (Para 259)

70.   All in all, the Government's commitment to furthering the work of the UN will
       require a commitment to creating a Foreign and Commonwealth Office for the
       twenty-first century which is equipped to undertake that necessary work. (Para
       260)

ANNEX A

OVERSEAS VISITS

I FORMER YUGOSLAVIA, CAMBODIA AND SOMALIA

Croatia (8–10 February 1993)

Members taking part: Mr David Howell, Mr David Harris, Mr Robert Wareing.

1. All the UN operations in the former Yugoslavia (UNPROFOR) were commanded and organised from Zagreb, including the humanitarian relief operations in Bosnia. Members met senior UN civilian and military personnel, including the head of UNHCR's operations, Mr Mendiluce. UNHCR was the lead agency for the humanitarian relief operation in Bosnia, to which UK troops were contributing. Committee members also met senior UK military personnel who were based in Bosnia, the British head of the EC Task force in Bosnia and a worker with a Dutch NGO operating in Bosnia. Meetings were also arranged with President Tudjman and with other leading politicians including the Vice President of the Serbian National Party of Croatia.

2. The visit did not inspire optimism for the future either of Croatia or Bosnia. UNPROFOR had not succeeded in demilitarising the UN Protected Areas (the Krajinas) in Croatia and negotiations in the south to permit Croatian access to the area east of the Maslenica bridge had broken down at the end of January. The situation in the Krajinas was very unstable. Paramilitary forces controlled by Serbia were perceived by Croatian politicians to be being protected by UNPROFOR and Serbia's borders with the Krajinas and with Bosnia were open. Elected Croatian Serb politicians had been threatened.

3. In Bosnia UNPROFOR had not been able to operate in Bosnian Serb controlled areas. Although many relief convoys were distributing food and other supplies in parts of Bosnia, convoys were in constant danger from armed groups. A relief flight from Zagreb to Sarajevo had been fired on just before the visit and during the visit the decision was taken to switch relief flights from Zagreb to Ancona in Italy.

4. All to whom the Committee spoke were pessimistic and believed the situation would get worse. Operations in former Yugoslavia were more complicated and difficult than any previous UN operations. High levels of hatred between the three communities in Bosnia and the ready availability of arms made implementation of UNPROFOR's mandate extremely difficult. There was also pessimism about the feasibility of the proposed settlement for Bosnia drawn up by Lord Owen and Mr Cyrus Vance.

Kosovo and Macedonia (8–10 February)

Members taking part: Sir John Stanley, Mr Dennis Canavan.

5. In the brief visit to these two parts of the former Yugoslavia, Members could not hope fully to understand the complex web of ethnic, religious and territorial disputes in which the area is enmeshed. Enough was learned to realise the immense difficulties facing the UN, or any other international organisation, in trying to bring stability to the region.

6. Kosovo, while regarded in Belgrade as the historic heartland of the Serbian people, has an overwhelmingly large Albanian population who, we were told, are continually harassed by the Serbian authorities. Members noted the effects of sanctions—long queues of cars at petrol stations. Members learned of the problems facing the UNHCR representative who was attempting—with two locally recruited assistants—to help the 7,000 refugees—about 3,000 Muslims and 4,000 Serbs—in the province. Not only were the Serbian authorities suspicious of UNHCR activities, but UNHCR staff were also accused of partiality by the local charities through which aid was delivered. This was partly because the UNHCR's implementing partner had been the local Red Cross which had been taken over by the Serbs and was accused of diverting supplies from needy Muslim refugees to Serbian refugees (and indeed to the war effort in Bosnia). One Muslim refugee from Bosnia told members of the Committee that, on arrival in Kosovo, he had been classed as a returnee rather than a refugee, as his family had lived in the area 100 years previously. He had been left with only his clothes, supplied by a charity in Croatia.

7. Members met the CSCE monitors in Pristina, whose mission is to promote dialogue between the Serbian and Albanian communities and to observe and report on the human rights situation and thereby attempt to improve it. They admitted to having made little progress in promoting dialogue between the two sides. However, Members were impressed by the monitors' work in pursuing alleged cases of human rights abuse. While they had no power to stop abuses of human rights themselves, they were able, by drawing attention to them, to alert CSCE member governments who could in turn put pressure on the Serbian government by formal and informal channels.

8. Discussion with leaders of the Albanian community and representatives of the Serbian authorities confirmed the pessimism of the CSCE observers as to bringing them together. The current Albanian leadership practise non-co-operation rather than overt resistance, and have elected their own "parliament" which has not yet met and has no powers. Albanians claimed that they were being systematically denied access to health care, education and other services; the authorities, on the other hand, laid the blame for the unemployment and increasing lack of primary healthcare on deliberate opting-out by the Albanian community. There was also a feeling in some quarters that the war might spread southwards, even if there were a ceasefire in Bosnia and Croatia—indeed, the more extreme nationalist elements might turn their attention to Kosovo once they had no further work to do in Bosnia.

9. Members also visited UN military observers at Pristina military airfield who were monitoring the air-exclusion zone. They collected information about the movements of all aircraft at the airfield and this information was passed to UNPROFOR in Belgrade. Similar teams were based at other airfields in the former Yugoslavia. Although they were only a small team and had had some problems with communications equipment, it was clear that they were performing a highly important task with great professionalism.

10. During the visit to Macedonia, the state was in the throes of a long-drawn-out campaign for recognition under that name in the face of vehement opposition from Greece. There was tension between nationalist and moderate elements over how far concessions should be made to Greek demands over the recognition issue, and also worries among the significant Albanian muslim minority about threats to their civil rights. All this was taking place against the background of a difficult economic situation due in part to the effects of the sanctions in place in respect of Serbia and Montenegro, and a Greek economic blockade.

11. President Gligorov emphasized that his government had invited the UNPROFOR contingent into the country to stop Macedonia becoming involved in the war in former Yugoslavia. The deployment and the reasons for it were generally accepted among other politicians. Members were impressed by the professional and efficient deployment of the troops, the first time UN forces had been deployed in advance of any potential conflict.

12. The overriding concerns at the time of the visit were the question of international recognition under a name including "Macedonia", the danger of the war spreading into Kosovo and Macedonia and the problems of tensions between ethnic groups in the country. The recognition question was important not just as a matter of national pride, but for security reasons: it was felt that as long as this issue remained unresolved, it left Macedonia open to the territorial ambitions of other states, while also making it impossible for the government to gain access to the resources of the IMF and other international bodies. This was vitally needed, as the war and the effects of sanctions were worsening the economic situation considerably. One CSCE monitor described Macedonia as being in the position of a good but empty house in a dangerous part of London. It was generally thought that recognition by the UN (which finally occurred on 8 April 1993) would alleviate the situation.

13. There were concerns among some people whom members met that troubles could arise in the area bordering Kosovo. "Incidents" would be manufactured or inflamed in the small Serbian communities in the villages near this border, which would give an excuse for intervention by Serbian forces. Both Albanian politicians and international observers told Members that the Albanian minority in Macedonia wanted neither to secede to Albania nor gain autonomy. Although they suffered some discrimination, there was nothing like the level of repression and human rights abuse present in Kosovo.

Cambodia (1–4 March 1993)

Members taking part: Mr Michael Jopling, Mr Dennis Canavan, Mr Jim Lester.

14. It was impressed on the Committee that the success or failure of the United Nations Transitional Authority in Cambodia (UNTAC) was a crucial test for the UN, especially given the failure of parties in Angola to respect the results of UN sponsored-elections there and the subsequent renewal of fighting. Despite signing the Paris Peace Agreement which led to the setting up of UNTAC, the Khmer Rouge had refused to disarm or to participate in elections. UNTAC had not been able to deploy troops in Khmer Rouge-controlled areas. UNTAC was the largest UN operation so far deployed and its presence dominated the streets of Phnom Penh.

15. A problem from the outset had been that the UN had not been sufficiently involved in the negotiations which led to the Paris Peace agreement. The Paris agreement—which was extremely ambitious in its scope—committed UNTAC to what was almost certainly an impossible mandate. UNTAC had taken too long to put together, and Mr Akashi, the Secretary General's Special Representative, had arrived before it was clear what the composition of UNTAC would be or when it would arrive. General Sanderson, the UN Force Commander, had had no say in the national composition of his force. He was, however, involved in the planning and logistics for the force in New York. French insistence on a bi-lin-

gual operation had contributed to delays in getting the operation going. There were problems of interpretation between different languages of UNTAC forces and personnel, but there was no shortage of
English/Khmer interpreters, many of whom were former refugees recruited from the camps in Thailand.

16. The repatriation by UNHCR of refugees from the camps in Thailand had been an enormous success and the Committee was extremely impressed by the exercise. 360,000 refugees had already been resettled and the last of the camps (Site Two) were to be closed and the occupants resettled before the
election. Members met some of the returnees at a camp near Battambang, their final staging post before
they began life on their own. Virtually all the refugees in the camps had wanted to return to Cambodia;
UNHCR was confident that the various political parties had not coerced them into returning to particular areas and most had been reunited with members of their families. Returnees mainly received cash and
building materials, together with a year's supply of food. The eventual handover from UNHCR to
UNDP (which are to take on long-term rehabilitation and development work) was still unclear. NGOs
had expressed concern that not all the resources pledged at the Tokyo conference in June 1992 for the
rebuilding of Cambodia had been translated into firm commitments.

17. Electoral registration, mainly carried out by UN volunteers, had been very successful; in some
areas over 100 per cent of the estimated eligible population had been registered. The high proportion of
electors registered lent some credence to Khmer Rouge claims of a continuing Vietnamese presence (the
grounds given for their non-participation in the election) and had led to claims by them that the UN had
not been acting impartially. Twenty parties had registered to take part in the election. In Phnom Penh
the Committee met senior representatives of the four main political parties and staff of the UNTAC electoral component, and visited the headquarters of the electoral operation. The main political parties taking part in the elections had established offices throughout the country and were about to begin the
campaign. There was little evidence of detailed political programmes.

18. Prince Sihanouk told Committee members that civil war would resume after the elections, and that
when UNTAC departed (planned for 25 August, three months after the election) he would call together
the three main parties to form a government of national reconciliation. He planned to set up a tripartite
administration, divide the country into three provinces, each governed by a triumvirate from the three
parties. He presumably intends to be the President. (No dates had been set for the Presidential election.
Powers of the President and the constitution are to be determined by the constituent assembly elected in
the elections). While stating that he would respect the results of the election he did not seem to think it
necessary for the eventual government to reflect the result and believed that a Khmer Rouge presence in
the government was inevitable, even though they were not taking part in the election.

19. The elections were being proceeded with although the essential first stage of the peace process
(cantonment of forces, demobilisation and disarming of factions) had failed because the Khmer Rouge
had stopped co-operating. Members concluded that it was likely the results of election would not be
respected by any of the parties, not just the Khmer Rouge and that the armies, particularly those of the
State of Cambodia (SOC) and Khmer Rouge, would resume the civil war (which had never in fact quite
stopped). Members were told during the visit that the UN in Mozambique, learning from the Cambodian
experience, were determined to ensure that phase two of the operation (the holding of elections) would
not automatically go ahead if phase one (the disarmament process) had not been successfully achieved.
UNTAC forces and personnel had not been adequately prepared for the problems they would face, especially the police contingent. There was no police adviser within the UN system.

20. There was widespread intimidation of voters by the political parties; most of this was thought to
be by SOC. The UN civilian police (CIVPOL) could not prevent this, although it was intended that
UNTAC troops would patrol routes to polling stations to try to ensure electors were not prevented from
voting. UNTAC had arrested some SOC people accused of political killings, who were awaiting trial. It
was not clear whether UNTAC actually had the authority to do this, nor how trials would be conducted.

21. The Committee was told that, were the civil war to break out again, no side had the military
capacity to win it, least of all the Khmer Rouge who controlled only 15 per cent of the country. Troops
of all sides only had the capacity for skirmishes, not battles. Troops were demoralised and SOC troops
were rarely paid, which had led to a high level of banditry and gangsterism. UN troops and monitors
tried to discourage illegal check-points by their patrols. But almost no revenue was being collected (the
UN presence in the civil administration seemed to have little effect) so troops and police unlikely to
start receiving salaries.

22. Members of the Committee met UN forces (including British officers) who formed part of naval
patrols on the Mekong river and in Battambang met military, police and civilian UN personnel. They
also met some of the many British NGOs working in Cambodia and visited a mine clearance operation
by the Halo Trust, a British charity, near the border with Thailand. UNTAC and NGOs are training
Cambodian mines clearance teams. Mines had been laid arbitrarily by all sides in the conflict and their
removal was likely to take many years.

23. Committee members travelled from Battambang, by road, to the Thai border. After meeting Thai troops rebuilding the road, the party crossed into Thailand by the bridge at Poipet, which is to be rebuilt by Thailand, funded by the UK. In Thailand the Committee had discussions with UNHCR and with government officials and politicians. Smuggling of logs and gemstones from Cambodia to Thailand provided forces in Cambodia, particularly the Khmer Rouge, with a source of income. Members were assured by Thai authorities that all border crossing points had been closed.

Somalia (1–4 March 1993)

Members taking part: Mr Ted Rowlands, Sir John Stanley and Mr Robert Wareing.

24. There were several parallels in Somalia with the situation in the Balkans. The UN is attempting to help bring about peace, stability, reconciliation and (eventually) reconstruction in a region of immensely complex ethnic divisions, which rarely coincide with the recognised international borders and have frequently led to armed conflict. In addition, this is a region with a long history of conflict and natural disasters. One result of the latter fact is that the humanitarian agencies, especially the non-governmental organisations (NGOs) have been active in the country for many years. Members of the Committee were very aware of this long-standing body of expertise during the visit, and the way the NGOs interacted with the UN was a running theme.

25. During the visit, the Committee gained the impression that the American-led airlift of food supplies (Operation Provide Relief) and the subsequent military intervention (Operation Restore Hope) had brought some improvement to the security situation, allowing a much greater level of food distribution to take place in the areas they visited. In Baidoa, for instance, the mortality rate had declined dramatically; in September 1992 6,000 dead bodies had been collected, in January 1992 the rate was only three or four a day. Nevertheless, the country had been devastated by the civil war, with hundreds of buildings destroyed and vast numbers of people displaced. The UN, UNITAF and the many relief agencies, with their many vehicles, aeroplanes and troops were ubiquitous.

26. Despite the overall improvement in the security situation, intermittent fighting was still going on in areas such as Kismayo and there were regular reports of attacks on UN, UNITAF and NGO staff across the country. Several workers with NGOs have been killed since the UNITAF deployment. Humanitarian workers were facing a greater risk of attack and the Committee were told by some that their organisations would have to consider withdrawing were more staff to be killed. Were there to be a large-scale withdrawal of NGO staff the relief effort in the country would be seriously affected. The Committee met many remarkable people working for the humanitarian organisations who were performing heroically often in very dangerous circumstances. Although there was concern about the level of security that could be provided, there seemed to be a good level of co-operation between the military forces of UNITAF and the NGO workers.

27. A key point that emerged from the visit was the widespread belief that the mandate and rules of engagement of the relaunched UNOSOM operation had to be as robust as those of the Unified Task Force (UNITAF). Military commanders doubted whether all those countries who had promised troops for the new operation would stand by their commitments were this not the case. Furthermore, the view of the military among others was that any military force in Somalia needed a devolved command structure and should not be "run from New York". The fear was also expressed that the Secretary General apparently proposed that UNOSOM should cover the whole country with a force no bigger than that which UNITAF used to cover only the south—this would have obvious implications for the UN's ability to maintain security. There was considerable doubt among NGOs, some UN agencies and (reportedly) the Somali population as to whether UNOSOM II would be able to maintain the level of security which UNITAF has achieved.

28. NGOs and some military personnel were often scathing about the lack of effective action by the UN agencies on the ground. There was a widespread feeling that the UN agencies had left the country when NGOs had stayed and now, having returned, were spending too long drafting programmes and not achieving practical results. In their defence, UN agencies argued that they were in the business of long-term rehabilitation; their job was to take over from the NGOs who were the ideal agencies for tackling immediate crises. NGOs and UN agencies agreed there was obvious merit in agreeing some such division of labour, as long as the UN delivered what it promised (which according to NGOs has not always been the case).

29. The Committee gained the impression that UNOSOM was active in Mogadishu but elsewhere had no more than a token representation, which lacked a clear mandate or real support from headquarters. In one case, the UNOSOM representative had even had to borrow a UN flag from the local UNITAF military commander. UNOSOM did not appear to be doing enough to advance the political work necessary for ensuring the long-term rehabilitation of the country. NGOs and the military had become involved in doing some of this work by default.

30. Although Somalia is recognised (not least in the Security Council Resolution 794 which authorised the deployment of UNITAF) as a unique case, if a UN force acting under Chapter VII to bring about ongoing relief and rehabilitation is seen to be successful, it was clear that there would be calls for similar forces to be deployed elsewhere. This would represent a significant change from the traditional practice of UN operations and would have substantial implications for the running of the UN and the demands membership would make on its member states.

31. On their way to Somalia, members of the Committee spent some time in Nairobi, where they were able to gain a Kenyan perspective on the crisis in Somalia and on East Africa in general. Meetings were also held with staff of the UN agencies working in Kenya, Sudan, Eritrea, Somalia and other countries in the region. The Kenyans were concerned at the prospect of continuing destabilisation caused by refugees and arms coming into their country from Somalia, which would exacerbate an already perilous economic situation. The UN agencies stressed that Somalia could not be seen in isolation: there had never been real peace in the Horn of Africa as a whole, with fighting between Somalia and Kenya, Somalia and Ethiopia and between Somalia and Northern Somalia ("Somaliland"). Furthermore, there were many other African countries which needed aid. For instance, Southern Sudan could become the next Somalia as far as the images on Western TV screens—which were a key impetus for public and governmental involvement—were concerned.

II LIST OF MEETINGS HELD DURING OVERSEAS VISITS

VISIT TO NEW YORK
9–12 November 1992

Members taking part: Mr David Howell, Mr Dennis Canavan, Mr Mike Gapes, Mr David Harris, Mr Michael Jopling, Mr Ted Rowlands, Mr Peter Shore, Sir John Stanley, Mr David Sumberg, Mr Robert Wareing.

Monday 9 November

HM Ambassador, Sir David Hannay, Permanent Representative to UN and UK Mission officials.

Mr Richard Kinchen, UKMIS

Tuesday 10 November

Mr Dick Thornburgh, Under Secretary General, Administration and Management Department.

HE Dr Boutros Boutros Ghali, Secretary General, United Nations.

HE Mrs Frechette, Permanent Representative, Canada, Mr Walter Maclean MP, Chairman, Committee on Development and Human Rights, Colonel Fraser, Canadian mission and staff of "Parliamentarians for Global Action".

Mr James Jonah, Under Secretary General, Political Affairs Department.

Mr Jan Eliasson, Under Secretary General, Department of Humanitarian Affairs.

Sir Michael Weston, Head of UK Delegation to the Conference on Disarmament, and Group Captain Paul Ryan, UK Delegation.

Wednesday 11 November

HE Mr Vorontsov, Permanent Representative, Russian Federation, and Professor Evgeniy Ambartsumov, Chairman, Foreign Relations Committee, Russian Parliament.

HE Mr Olara Otunnu, International Peace Academy, and Mr F.T. Liu, International Peace Academy.

HE Mr Wisnumurti, Permanent Representative, Indonesia.

Thursday 12 November

Mr Elaraby (Permananent Representative, Egypt), Chairman of the General Assembly Informal Working Group on Agenda for Peace.

Mr Ganev, President of the General Assembly.

HE Mr Ed Perkins, Permanent Representative, USA.

Mr Kofi Annan, Assistant Secretary General, Mr Hedi Annabi and Mr Joachim Hutter, Peacekeeping Department.

General Petrovsky, Under Secretary General, Political Affairs Department.

HE Mr Jean-Bernard Merimee, Permanent Representative, France.

HE Mr Hatano, Permanent Representative, Japan.

VISIT TO FORMER YUGOSLAVIA

7–10 February 1993

CROATIA (ZAGREB)

Members taking part: Mr Howell, Mr Harris, Mr Wareing.

Monday 8 February

General Godreau, Deputy UNPROFOR Force Commander.

Mr Cedric Thornberry, Director of Civil Affairs UNPROFOR.

Mr Jose Maria Mendiluce, UNHCR Special Representative.

Lt Colonel Maxwell, Liaison Officer UNPROFOR/UNHCR.

Tuesday 9 February

Mr Milan Ducik, Vice-President of the Serbian National Party of Croatia.

Mr Milas, Deputy Prime Minister.

President Franjo Tujman.

Mr Zarko Domljan, Chairman of the Foreign Affairs Committee, Croatian Parliament and members of the Committee.

Mr Nils Rosdahl, Deputy Special Representative, WHO.

Mr David McAdam, WHO.

Mr Thomas McDermott, Special Representative, UNICEF.

Mr David Morton, World Food Programme Director.

Mr Louis Montsma, Logistical Adviser, Medecins sans Frontieres.

7–10 February 1993

MACEDONIA AND KOSOVO

Members taking part: Sir John Stanley, Mr Canavan.

Monday 8 February

Mr Bjorn Wakman, UNHCR, Field Officer.

Staff of the Merhamet charity.

Dr Milos Simovic, Head of Kosovo District Administration.

Dr Ibrahim Rugova, Democratic League of Kosovo.

Mr Philipp Hahn, CSCE Monitoring Mission, and colleagues.

Dr Richardt Vork, Director, EC Sanctions Assistance Mission.

Tuesday 9 February

President Gligorov.

Mr Andrew Roberts, UN Civilian Office, Skopje.

Ambassador Whitman, CSCE Spillover Mission.

Professor Sami Ibrahimi, Vice President, Party for Democratic Prosperity.

Mr Lupco Georgievski, President, Macedonian Internal Revolutionary Party.

Mr Todor Malanovski, Under Secretary of State, Ministry of Defence.

Wednesday 10 February

Mr Stopan Andov, President of the Assembly.

VISIT TO GENEVA

11 February 1993

Members taking part: Mr Howell, Mr Canavan, Mr Harris, Sir John Stanley, Mr Wareing.

Thursday 11 February

Mr F Fouanit, Head of UNHCR Task Force in Yugoslavia.

Mrs Sadata Ogata, UN High Commissioner for Refugees.

Mr Werner Blatter, Director of the UNHCR Asia Bureau, and Mr Andrew Mayne, Desk Office Cambodia, UNHCR.

Mr Lamuniere and Mr Boule, Department of Humanitarian Affairs.

Colonel Messervy-Whiting, Military Adviser to Lord Owen.

Mr Cornelio Sommaruga, President, International Committee of the Red Cross.

Mr Vincente Berasetyin, Secretary General, Conference on Disarmament.

VISIT TO CAMBODIA AND THAILAND

Members taking part: Mr Michael Jopling, Mr Dennis Canavan, Mr Jim Lester.

28 February–3 March 1993

PHNOM PENH

Sunday 28 February

HM Ambassador Mr David Burns.

Lt Col N Mulliner, Commander, British contingent UNTAC

Commander John Leighton, RM, UNTAC.

Lt Col A Duncan, R Signals, UNTAC

Monday 1 March

HE Mr Hor Nam Hong, Foreign Minister, Member of the Supreme National Council.

Mr Chan Youran, PDK.

Lt Col Dick Palk UNTAC, Military Public Information Office.

HRH Prince Norodom Sihanouk.

Mr Sergio Vieira de Mello, Director of UNTAC Repatriation Component.

Mr Ieng Mouly, (BDLP) Member of SNC.

Mr Yasushi Akashi, UN Secretary General's Special Representative.

Staff of UK non-governmental organisations working in Phnom Penh.

Tuesday 2 March

Lt Gen John Sanderson, UNTAC Force Commander.

Mr Michael Maley, Deputy Director of the Electoral Component of UNTAC.

Mr Sam Rainsy, (FUNCINPEC) Member of the SNC.

Col Ashad, UNTAC Sector 8 Commander.

Col Manfred Bliem, UNTAC Director, Civil Police (CIVPOL), Section 8.

Mr Mocef Khane, Officer in Charge, UNTAC Provincial Headquarters.

Mr Udo Janz, Head of UNHCR Sub Office, Battambeng.

Mr Andrew Bouchard, UNTAC electoral officer Battambang.

Staff of UK non-governmental organisations working in Battambang.

Wednesday 3 March

    Otaki Repatriation Centre.

    Halo Trust Mine Clearance team at Sophi.

    Thai Batallion Headquarters, Poipet.

THAILAND

    Jahanshah Assadi, Head of Sub-Office UNHCR, Aranyaprathet.

Thursday 4 March.

    General Charan Kullavanijaya, Secretary General, National Security Council.

    Mrs Colchineepan Chiranond, Deputy Director, Department of East Asian Affairs.

    Members of the Foreign Affairs Committee of the Thai Parliament.

    Mr Refeuddin Ahmed, UN Under Secretary General, ESCAP.

    Major General Teerawat Putamanonda, Director of Army Intelligence, Royal Thai Army.

VISIT TO NAIROBI AND SOMALIA

1–4 March 1993

    Members taking part: Sir John Stanley, Mr Ted Rowlands, Mr Robert Wareing.

NAROBI

Monday 1 March

    Sir Kieran Prendergast, British High Commissioner, Nairobi.

    Mr S Muchilwa, Minister of State, Ministry of Foreign Affairs.

    Dr Sally Kosgei, Ministry of Foreign Affairs.

    Hon Kipkalya Kones, Minister of State and Mr Wilfred Kimalat, Permanent Secretary, office of the President.

    Members of the UN Disaster Management Team, (UNHCR, UNICEF, WFP).

    UNDP representatives from Kenya, Somalia, Sudan, Djibouti, Eritrea and Ethiopia.

SOMALIA

BAIDOA

Tuesday 2 March

    Mr Paul Oberson, International Committee of the Red Cross(ICRC).

    Mr Patric Vercammen, UNOSOM.

    Major Richard Stanhope, UNITAF.

MOGADISHU

    Ambassador Ismat Kittani, Secretary General's Special Representative.

Wednesday 3 March

    Mr Mark Stirling, UNICEF.

    Nina Winquist, ICRC.

    Mr Steve Rifkin, Save the Children, and representatives of other NGOs.

    Colonel Mellor, Royal Australian Regiment.

    Brigadier-General Cox, Chief of Staff, UNOSOM II

    Mr John Hirsch, US Charge d'Affaires, and General Johnston, UNITAF.

    Mr Peter Schumann, UNDP

    Staff of UN agencies in Mogadishu.

BELET HUEN

Thursday 4 March

Major Rod Mackay, Canadian forces.

Mr Kevin Hopkins, SCF (UK).

Mr Pascal Mauchle, ICRC.

ANNEX B

INFORMAL MEETINGS OF THE COMMITTEE

3 September 1992

Hon Lloyd Axworthy MP, Opposition Spokesman for External Affairs, Canada

4 September 1992

Senor Paul Roa, Vice Foreign Minister, Cuba

21 September 1992

Rt Hon Lord Owen

22 September 1992

Mr Nozawa, Japanese Senate Foreign Affairs Committee

3 November 1992

HE Mr Boris Pankin, Ambassador of the Russian Federation

19 November 1992

HE The Hon Raymond G H Seitz, Ambassador of the United States

24 November 1992

Rt Hon Mohamed Abdelaziz, President of Polisario, Western Sahara

25 November 1992

Mr W H Fullerton CMG, HM Ambassador to Kuwait

1 December 1992

Mr John Struan Robertson, Chairman, New Zealand Foreign Affairs and Defence Select Committee

9 December 1992

Mr Jawhar Namiq Salem, Mr Sadi Pire, Dr Hama-Najm Hassan and Mr Francis Yousif Shabo, Members of the Iraqi-Kurdish Parliament

14 January 1993

Mr Desimir Tosic, representative of President Cosic of Yugoslavia

26 January 1993

Mr Sergei Stepashin, Mr Aleksandr Piskunov and other members of the Defence and Security Committee of the Supreme Soviet, Russian Federation

Mr Anton Vasiliev, Deputy Chief, First Department of the Asia-Pacific Region, Russian Ministry of Foreign Affairs

1 February 1993

HE Mr Mohamed I Shaker, Ambassador of Egypt, HE Mr Fouad Ayoub, Ambassador of Jordan, HE Mr Mahmoud Hammoud, Ambassador of Lebanon, HE Mr Mohammad Khodor, Ambassador of Syria and Mr Afif Safia, PLO Representative in London

2 February 1993

HE Mr Seyoum Mesfin, Minister of Foreign Affairs, Ethiopia

19 February 1993

Dr Esmaeel Al Shatti, Dr Nasser Al Sane and Mr Abdul Al Samed, Members of the Financial and Economic Committee and Mr Al Duwaillah, Chairman of the POWs Committee, Kuwait National Assembly

5 February 1993

Mr Dennis McNamara, Director of the Human Rights Component, UNTAC

11 March 1993

Mr Svetozar Stojanovic, Principal Adviser to President Cosic of Yugoslavia

16 March 1993

Mr C L Sharma, Senior Special Adviser to the Director General, UNESCO

17 March 1993

HE Mr Teodor Melescanu, Deputy Prime Minister and Minister of Foreign Affairs, Romania

23 March 1993

Mr Irvin Hicks, US Ambassador to the United Nations

Mr Glafcos Clerides, President of the Republic of Cyprus

29 April 1993

Dr Haris Siladjic, Bosnian Foreign Minister

4 May 1993

Sir David Hannay KCMG, UK Permanent Representative to the United Nations

17 May 1993

Dr Adrian Nastase, President of the Chamber of Deputies of the Romanian Parliament

18 May 1993

Members of the European Affairs Committee, Bundestag, Federal Republic of Germany

8 June 1993

Members of the Standing Committee on Foreign Affairs, Thailand.

ANNEX C

AN AGENDA FOR PEACE

SUMMARY OF THE SECRETARY GENERAL'S PROPOSALS

(An Agenda for Peace contains a large number of conclusions, proposals and recommendations which are difficult to tabulate in a definitive form. The following list includes all the main conclusions and recommendations of the Secretary General's report.)

Preventive diplomacy

Confidence-building measures

1. All regional organisations should consider what further confidence-building measures might be applied in their areas and to inform the United Nations of the results (para 24).

2. The Secretary General will undertake periodic consultations on confidence-building measures with parties to potential, current or past disputes (para 24).

Fact-finding

3. A request by a state for the sending of a UN fact-finding mission to its territory should be considered by the Security Council without delay (para 25).

4. All member states should be ready to provide the information needed for effective preventive diplomacy (para 25).

5. In exceptional circumstances, the Security Council should meet away from New York (as provided for in the Charter) in order to inform itself directly and to bring the authority of the UN to bear on a given situation (para 25).

Early warning

6. There is a need to strengthen the UN's early warning arrangements on environmental and humanitarian threats and co-ordinate them with sources of political information (para 26).

7. The Economic and Social Council (ECOSOC) should provide reports on economic and social developments that may threaten international peace and security (para 26).

8. Regional organisations which do not already have observer status at the UN should apply for it and be linked into the security mechanisms of the UN (para 27).

Preventive deployment

9. Preventive deployment within a state, in conditions of national crisis, could take place with the consent of the government and parties concerned (para 28).

10. Preventive deployment should be authorised on the borders of states, with their consent, where this would remove the likelihood of hostilities between states (para 31).

11. Preventive deployment along one side of a border in similar circumstances where it would serve to deter conflict (para 32).

Demilitarised zones

12. Consideration should be given to the establishment of demilitarised zones as a form of preventive deployment on each side of a border with the consent of the states concerned, or on one side only at the request of one party (para 33).

Peacemaking

13. The Security Council should take full advantage of the provisions of the Charter under which it may recommend appropriate procedures or methods for dispute settlement and make recommendations to the parties for a peaceful settlement of the dispute.

14. It is essential to promote the utilization of the General Assembly by all member states so as to bring greater influence to bear in pre-empting or containing situations which are likely to threaten international peace and security (para 36).

15. The Secretary General will continue to use distinguished statesmen as mediators and facilitators in his "good offices" work; this work is often best carried out independently of the deliberative bodies of the UN (para 37).

The World Court

16. The Secretary General should be authorised to seek advisory opinions from the International Court of Justice; and other UN organs should use it more frequently (para 38).

17. All member states should accept the general jurisdiction of the Court by the year 2000 (para 39).

18. Member states should support the Trust Fund established to assist countries which are unable to meet the cost of bringing cases to the Court (para 39).

Amelioration through assistance

19. The UN should be able to draw on the resources of all its agencies and programmes to facilitate peacemaking by means of action to ameliorate the circumstances which contribute to the dispute or conflict; the inter-agency system should improve its contribution to the peaceful resolution of disputes (para 40).

Sanctions

20. The Security Council should devise a set of measures to insulate states confronted with economic difficulties due to sanctions from such economic difficulties (para 41).

Use of military force

21. The Security Council should initiate negotiations—with the assistance of the Military Staff Committee—to establish agreements with member states for the provision on a permanent basis of armed forces (para 43).

Peace-enforcement units

22. The Security Council should consider the utilisation of peace-enforcement units, consisting of volunteer troops more heavily armed than peacekeeping forces, which would ensure compliance with ceasefires—a task which can on occasion "exceed the mission of peacekeeping forces" (para 44).

Peacekeeping

Increasing demands

23. The Secretary General strongly supports proposals for peacekeeping contributions to be financed from defence rather than foreign affairs budgets (para 48).

Personnel

24. Member states should make stand-by arrangements with the UN for the provision of skilled personnel they would be prepared to offer to the Organisation (para 51).

25. Arrangements for the training of peacekeeping personnel should be reviewed and improved using the capabilities of the UN, NGOs and member states; e.g. member states with considerable potential should focus on language training for police personnel (para 52)

26. The UN should institute special personnel procedures to permit the rapid transfer of secretariat staff to service with peacekeeping operations (para 52)

27. The strength and capability of military staff serving in the Secretariat should be augmented to meet new and heavier requirements (para 52).

Logistics

28. A pre-positioned stock of basic peacekeeping equipment should be established (vehicles, communications equipment, generators etc); alternatively member states should commit themselves to keeping such equipment on stand-by for use by the UN (para 53).

29. Member states in a position to do so should make air- and sea-lift capacity available to the UN free of cost or at lower than commercial rates (para 54).

Post-conflict peacebuilding

30. The UN should develop and provide technical assistance for transforming deficient national structures and capabilities of states, and for the strengthening of new democratic institutions (para 59).

Co-operation with regional arrangements

31. Regional arrangements and agencies can render great service if they act in a manner consistent with the Charter (para 63).

32. Regional action as a matter of decentralisation, delegation and co-operation with UN efforts could lighten the burden of the Security Council and contribute to a deeper sense of participation in international affairs (para 64).

Safety of UN personnel

33. The Security Council should gravely consider what action should be taken towards those who put UN personnel in danger; the Council should consider in advance of deployment the possibility of using measures under Chapter VII were the UN operation to be systematically frustrated and hostilities occur.

Financing

The previous Secretary General's proposals, with which Dr Boutros Ghali is in "broad agreement"

34. Interest should be charged on outstanding assessed contributions (para 70).

35. Budgetary surpluses should be allowed to be retained (para 70).

36. The Working Capital Fund should be increased to $250 million (para 70).

37. A peacekeeping reserve fund of $50 million should be established to meet initial expenses of peacekeeping operations (para 70).

38. The Secretary General should be authorized to borrow commercially (para 70).

39. A humanitarian revolving fund of $50 million should be established for emergency humanitarian situations (para 70). (This has been agreed to.)

40. A UN peace endowment fund of $1 billion should be established (para 70).

The current Secretary General's additional proposals

41. Member states must pay their assessed contributions in full and on time (para 72).

42. One-third of the estimated cost of each new peace-keeping operation should be appropriated by the General Assembly as soon as the Security Council decides to establish an operation (para 73).

43. The Secretary General should have the authority to place contracts without competitive bidding in exceptional circumstances (para 73).

An Agenda for Peace

44. Heads of state and government of the members of the Security Council should meet every other year; and it should continue to meet at foreign minister level (para 79).

45. The Secretary General is taking steps to rationalize and in certain cases integrate the various programmes and agencies of the UN within specific countries. The senior UN official should serve as the Secretary General's representative on matters of particular concern.

ANNEX D

UN PEACE-KEEPING AND OBSERVER MISSIONS

A. United Nations Peace-keeping Operations established before 1987

1.　　　United Nations Truce Supervision Organisation **(UNTSO)**
1948 to present.
Egypt, Israel, Jordan, Lebanon and Syria.
Authority and Mandate: Security Council: supervision of truce in 1948, supervision of General Armistice Agreements of 1949, ceasefires in the Suez and Golan Heights, and assistance to UNIFIL and UNDOF.
Maximum personnel: 572 (1948)
Fatalities: 28

2.　　　United Nations Military Observer Group in India and Pakistan **(UNMOGIP)**
1949 to present.
Authority and Mandate: Security Council: supervision of the ceasefire between India and Pakistan in Jammu and Kashmir.
Maximum personnel: 102 (1965)
Fatalities: 6

3.　　　United Nations Emergency Force **(UNEF I)**
1956–67
First in the Suez sector and the Sinai peninsula. Then along the Gaza area and the international frontier in the Sinai peninsula on the Egyptian side only.
Authority and mandate: General Assembly: to secure and supervise the cessation of hostilities, including the withdrawal of the armed forces of France, Israel and the United Kingdom from Egypt territory, and after the withdrawal to serve as a buffer between the Egyptian and Israeli forces.
Maximum strength: 6,073 (February 1957)
Fatalities: 90

4.　　　United Nations Observation Group in Lebanon **(UNOGIL)**
1958
Authority and Mandate: Security Council: to ensure that there was no illegal infiltration of personnel of supply of arms or other material across the Lebanon borders.
Maximum size: 591 (November 1958)

5.　　　United Nations Operation in the Congo **(ONUC)**
July 1960 to June 1964
Authority and Mandate: Security Council: to ensure the withdrawal of Belgian forces, to assist the Government in maintaining law and order and to provide technical assistance: to maintain the territorial integrity and the political independence of the Congo, to prevent the occurrence of

civil war, and to secure the removal from the Congo of all foreign military, paramilitary and advisory personnel not under the United Nations command, and all mercenaries.
Maximum strength: 19,828 (July 1961)
Fatalities: 234

6.   United Nations Security Force in West New Guinea (West Irian) **(UNSF)**
October 1962 to April 1963
Authority and Mandate: General Assembly: to maintain peace and security in the territory under the United Nations Temporary Executive Authority (UNTEA) established by agreement between Indonesia and the Netherlands.
Maximum strength: 1,500 infantry personnel and 76 aircraft personnel.

7.   United Nations Yemen Observation Mission **(UNYOM)**
July 1963 to September 1964
Authority and Mandate: Security Council: to observe and certify the implementation of the disengagement agreement between Saudi Arabia and the United Arab Republic.
Maximum strength: 25 military observers;
                 114 officers and other ranks of a reconnaissance unit;
                 50 officers and other ranks of an air unit.

8.   United Nations Peace-keeping Force in Cyprus **(UNFICYP)**
March 1964 to present
Authority and Mandate: Security Council: in the interest of preserving international peace and security, to use its best efforts to prevent the recurrence of fighting and, as necessary, to contribute to the maintenance and restoration of law and order and a return to normal conditions. Since 1974 this has included supervising the ceasefire and maintaining a buffer zone between the lines of the Cyprus National Guard and of the Turkish and the Turkish Cypriot forces.
Maximum strength: 6,411 (June 1964)
Fatalities: 159

9.   Mission of the Representative of the Secretary-General in the Dominican Republic **(DOMREP)**
May 1965 to October 1966
Authority and Mandate: Security Council: to observe the situation and to report on breaches of the ceasefire between the two *de facto* authorities.
Maximum strength: 2 military observers

10.   United Nations India-Pakistan Observation Mission **(UNIPOM)**
September 1965 to March 1966
Authority and Mandate: Security Council: to supervise the ceasefire along the India/Pakistan border except in the State of Jammu and Kashmir where UNMOGIP operated, and the withdrawal of all armed personnel to the positions held by them before 5 August 1965.
Maximum strength: 96 military observers (October 1965)

11.   Second United Nations Emergency Force **(UNEF II)**
October 1973 to July 1979
Suez Canal and later the Sinai peninsula
Authority and Mandate: Security Council: to supervise the ceasefire between Egyptian and Israeli forces and, following the conclusion of the agreements of 18 January 1974 and 4 September 1975, to supervise the redeployment of Egyptian and Israeli forces and to man and control the buffer zones established under those agreements.
Maximum strength: 6,973 (February 1974)
Fatalities: 52

12.   United Nations Disengagement Observation Force **(UNDOF)**
June 1974 to present
Syrian Golan Heights
Authority and Mandate: Security Council: to supervise the ceasefire between Israel and Syria; to supervise the redeployment of Syrian armed forces; and to establish a buffer zone as provided in the Agreement on Disengagement between Israeli and Syrian forces of 31 May 1974.
Maximum strength: 1,450
Fatalities: 31

13.   United Nations Interim Force in Southern Lebanon **(UNIFIL)**
March 1978 to present
Authority and Mandate: Security Council: to confirm the withdrawal of Israeli forces from Southern Lebanon, to restore international peace and security and to assist the Government of Lebanon in ensuring the return of its effective authority in the area.
Maximum strength: 7,000
Fatalities: 190

B. PEACE-KEEPING OPERATIONS ESTABLISHED BEFORE 1987: COSTS IN CASH TERMS TO JANUARY 1993 AND
METHOD OF FINANCE

UNIFIL	$	2,059,382,450	(Special Peace-keeping Account)
UNFICYP	$	691,400,000	(Voluntary Contributions)
UNDOF	$	525,467,000	(Special Peace-keeping Account)
UNEF II	$	446,487,000	(Special Peace-keeping Account)
ONUC	$	400,130,793	(Special Peace-keeping Account)
UNTSO	$	372,521,300	(Regular Budget)
UNEF I	$	214,249,000	(Special Peace-keeping Account)
UNMOGIP	$	81,709,000	(Regular Budget)
UNOGIL	$	3,697,000	(Regular Budget)
UNYOM	$	1,840,000	(States sharing costs in equal parts)
UNIPOM	$	1,713,280	(Regular Budget)
DOMREP	$	275,831	(Regular Budget
UNSF	$	costs unknown	(States sharing costs in equal parts)

C. GEOGRAPHICAL DISTRIBUTION OF PEACE-KEEPING OPERATIONS ESTABLISHED BEFORE 1987

Africa:
   ONUC

Asia:
   UNSF

Central America:
   DOMREP

Indian Subcontinent:
   UNMOGIP
   UNIPOM

Middle Fast:
   UNTSO
   UNEF I
   UNOGIL
   UNYOM
   UNFICYP
   UNEF II
   UNDOF
   UNIFIL

D. UNITED NATIONS PEACE-KEEPING OPERATIONS ESTABLISHED SINCE 1987

1. Afghanistan/Pakistan   **UNGOMAP**: UN Good Offices Mission in Afghanistan and Pakistan
                           (April 1988–March 1990) 50 military observers.

2. Angola   **UNAVEM I**: UN Angola Verification Mission (January 1989–June 1991) 70
                           military observers.

3. Angola   **UNAVEM II**: UN Angola Verification Mission (June 1991–present) 350
                           military observers, air section and 90 police.

4. Cambodia   **UNAMIC**: UN Advanced Mission in Cambodia (October 1991–March
                           1992) 380 military and civilian personnel.

5. Cambodia   **UNTAC**: UN Transitional Authority in Cambodia (March 1992–present)
                           19,000–20,000 military, civilian and police personnel.

6. Central America   **ONUCA**: UN Observer Group in Central America (November
                           1989–January 1992) 1,098 military observers and armed soldiers and naval
                           personnel.

7. El Salvador   **ONUSAL**: UN Observer Mission in El Salvador (July 1991–present) 135
                           civilian, police and military.

8. Iran-Iraq   **UNIIMOG**: UN Iran-Iraq Military Observer Group (August 1988–June
                           1991) 399 military observers.

9. Iraq-Kuwait   **UNIKOM**: UN Iraq-Kuwait Observation Mission (April 1991–present) 300
                           military observers and 550 UN armed soldiers for first three months.

10. Mozambique   **ONUMOZ**: United Nations Mission in Mozambique (December 1992–present) approximately 8,000 military planned.

11. Namibia   **UNTAG**: UN Transition Assistance Group in Namibia (April 1989–March 1990) 4,650 military, 450 civilian, 1,350 election staff and 1,500 police.

12. Somalia   **UNOSOM**: UN Operation in Somalia (April 1992–May 1993) 50 military observers, 500 UN armed soldiers.

13. Somalia   **UNOSOM II**: UN Operation in Somalia (which took over from Unified Task Force (UNITAF)) (May 1993–present) 28,000 armed soldiers, 2,000 civilians.

14. Western Sahara   **MINURSO**: UN Mission for the Referendum in Western Sahara (September 1991–present) 1,700 military observers, 450 civilian electoral staff and 300 police.

15. Yugoslavia   **UNPROFOR**: UN Protection Force (March 1992-present) over 20,000 soldiers, military observers, police and civilians.

E. UNITED NATIONS OBSERVER ETC MISSIONS ESTABLISHED SINCE 1987

1. Afghanistan/Pakistan   **OSGAP**: Office of the Secretary-General in Afghanistan and Pakistan (1990–present) personal representative and 10 military observers.

2. Central America   **CIAV**: UN/OAS International Commission of Support and Verification (1989) 150 civilians.

3. Haiti   **ONUVEH**: UN Observer Mission to verify the electoral process in Haiti (1990–1991) 250 civilians and a small number of military observers.

4. Iraq   UN Civilian Guards (1991–present) 500 maximum.

5. Nicaragua   **ONUVEN**: UN Observer Mission to verify the electoral process in Nicaragua (1989–1990) 207 civilian observers.

PROCEEDINGS OF THE COMMITTEE
RELATING TO THE REPORT

TUESDAY 22 JUNE 1993

Members present:

Mr David Howell, in the Chair

Mr Dennis Canavan	Mr Peter Shore
Mr Mike Gapes	Sir John Stanley
Mr Michael Jopling	Mr David Sumberg
Mr Ted Rowlands	Mr Robert N. Wareing

The Committee deliberated.

Draft Report, proposed by the Chairman, [The Expanding Rôle of the United Nations and its Implications for United Kingdom Policy] brought up and read.

Ordered, That the Chairman's draft Report be read a second time, paragraph by paragraph.

Paragraph 1 postponed.

Paragraphs 2 and 3 read, amended and agreed to.

Paragraphs 4 to 11 read and agreed to.

Paragraph 12 read, amended and agreed to.

Paragraphs 13 to 21 read and agreed to.

Paragraph 22 read, amended and agreed to.

Paragraphs 23 and 24 read and agreed to.

Paragraph 25 read amended and agreed to.

Paragraphs 26 and 27 read and agreed to.

Paragraph 28 read, amended and agreed to.

Paragraphs 29 to 32 read and agreed to.

Paragraph 33 read, amended and agreed to.

Paragraphs 34 to 38 read and agreed to.

Paragraphs 39 and 40 read, amended and agreed to.

Paragraphs 41 and 42 read and agreed to.

Paragraph 43 read, amended and agreed to.

Paragraphs 44 to 49 read and agreed to.

Paragraph 50 read, amended and agreed to.

Paragraphs 51 to 53 read and agreed to.

Paragraphs 54 and 55 read, amended and agreed to.

Paragraphs 56 to 60 read and agreed to.

Paragraph 61 read, amended and agreed to.

Paragraph 62 read and agreed to.

Paragraph 63 read, amended and agreed to.

Paragraph 64 read and agreed to.

Paragraph 65 read, amended and agreed to.

Paragraph 66 read and agreed to.

Paragraph 67 read, amended and agreed to.

Paragraphs 68 to 70 read and agreed to.

Paragraph 71 read, amended and agreed to.

Paragraph 72 read and agreed to.

Paragraphs 73 and 74 read, amended and agreed to.

Paragraph 75 read and agreed to.

Paragraphs 76 to 78 read, amended and agreed to.

Paragraph 79 read and agreed to.

Paragraph 80 read, amended and agreed to.

Paragraph 81 read and agreed to.

Paragraphs 82 and 83 read, amended and agreed to.

Paragraph 84 read and agreed to.

Paragraph 85 read, amended and agreed to.

Paragraphs 86 to 88 read and agreed to.

Paragraph 89 read, amended and agreed to.

Paragraphs 90 and 91 read and agreed to.

Paragraph 92 read, amended and agreed to.

Paragraph 93 read and agreed to.

Paragraphs 94 to 96 read, amended and agreed to.

Paragraph 97 read and agreed to.

Paragraph 98 read, amended and agreed to.

Paragraphs 99 and 100 read and agreed to.

Paragraph 101 read, amended and agreed to.

Paragraph 102 read and agreed to.

Paragraph 103 read, amended and agreed to.

Paragraph 104 read and agreed to.

Paragraph 105 read, amended and agreed to.

Paragraphs 106 to 109 read and agreed to.

Paragraph 110 read, amended and agreed to.

Paragraph 111 read and agreed to.

Paragraph 112 read, amended and agreed to.

Paragraphs 113 to 117 read and agreed to.

Paragraph 118 read, amended and agreed to.

A paragraph—(*Sir John Stanley.*)—brought up, read the first and second time and inserted
(now paragraph 119).

Paragraph 119 (now paragraph 120) read and agreed to.

Paragraph 120 (now paragraph 121) read, amended and agreed to.

Paragraphs 121 to 128 (now paragraphs 122 to 129) read and agreed to.

Paragraphs 129 and 130 (now paragraphs 130 and 131) read, amended and agreed to.

Ordered, That further consideration of the Chairman's draft Report be now adjourned.—(*The Chairman.*)

Report to be further considered tomorrow.

[Adjourned till tomorrow at Ten o'clock.

WEDNESDAY 23 JUNE 1993
[MORNING SESSION]
Members present:

Mr David Howell, in the Chair

Mr Dennis Canavan   Mr Peter Shore
Mr Mike Gapes   Sir John Stanley
Mr Michael Jopling   Mr David Sumberg
Mr Jim Lester   Mr Robert N Wareing
Mr Ted Rowlands

The Committee deliberated.

Consideration of the Chairman's draft Report resumed.

Paragraphs 131 and 132 (now paragraphs 132 and 133) read and agreed to.

Paragraphs 133 to 135 (now paragraphs 134 to 136) read, amended and agreed to.

Paragraphs 136 and 137 (now paragraphs 137 and 138) read and agreed to.

Paragraph 138 (now paragraph 139) read, amended and agreed to.

Paragraph 139 (now paragraph 140) read and agreed to.

Paragraph 140 (now paragraph 141) read, amended and agreed to.

Paragraph 141 read, as follows:

"In **Iraq**, aircraft of the coalition forces have enforced an air-exclusion zone in pursuance of SCR 688. Aircraft violating the zone have been shot down (13 and 18 January 1993), aircraft of the coalition have attacked Iraqi air defence facilities and command and control facilities. On 17 January, American cruise missiles were used pursuant to SCR 687 to attack a facility connected with the Iraqi weapons of mass destruction programme. The action against the weapons facility was confirmed by the Secretary-General to be within the mandate of SCR 688, but that resolution has taken the UN into disputed territory."

An Amendment made.

Another Amendment proposed, in line 5, after the word "programme" to insert the words "but innocent people were tragically killed as a result".—(*Mr Dennis Canavan.*)

Question put That the Amendment be made.

The Committee divided.

Ayes, 1   Noes, 5

Mr Dennis Canavan   Mr Michael Jopling
                                 Mr Jim Lester
                                 Mr Ted Rowlands
                                 Mr Peter Shore
                                 Sir John Stanley

Another Amendment made.

Paragraph (now paragraph 142) as amended, agreed to.

Paragraph 142 (now paragraph 143) read, amended and agreed to.

Paragraphs 143 to 145 (now paragraphs 144 to 146) read and agreed to.

Paragraph 146 (now paragraph 147) read, amended and agreed to.

Paragraph 147 (now paragraph 148) read and agreed to.

Paragraph 148 (now paragraph 149) read, amended and agreed to.

Paragraphs 149 to 157 (now paragraphs 150 to 158) read and agreed to.

Paragraph 158 (now paragraph 159) read, amended and agreed to.

Paragraph 159 (now paragraph 160) read and agreed to.

Paragraph 160 (now paragraph 161) read, amended and agreed to.

Paragraph 161 (now paragraph 162) read and agreed to.

Paragraph 162 (now paragraph 163) read, amended and agreed to.

Paragraphs 163 to 172 (now paragraphs 164 to 173) read and agreed to.

Paragraphs 173 and 174 (now paragraphs 174 and 175) read, amended and agreed to.

Paragraphs 175 to 177 (now paragraphs 176 to 178) read and agreed to.

Paragraph 178 (now paragraph 179) read, amended and agreed to.

Paragraphs 179 to 184 (now paragraphs 180 to 185) read and agreed to.

Paragraphs 185 and 186 (now paragraphs 186 and 187) read, amended and agreed to.

Paragraphs 187 to 189 (now paragraphs 188 to 190) postponed.

A paragraph—(*Mr Mike Gapes.*)—brought up, and read, as follows:

"However we believe the British Government should not simply block proposals for enlarging the Security Council, but should urgently bring forward its own proposals for reform. If it does not, it risks being outflanked by an alliance of other countries including the USA."

Question put, That the paragraph be read a second time.

The Committee divided.

Ayes, 3	Noes, 6
Mr Dennis Canavan	Mr Michael Jopling
Mr Mike Gapes	Mr Jim Lester
Mr Robert N Wareing	Mr Ted Rowlands
	Mr Peter Shore
	Sir John Stanley
	Mr David Sumberg

Postponed paragraphs 187 and 188 (now paragraphs 188 and 189) read, amended and agreed to.

Postponed paragraph 189 (now paragraph 190) read and agreed to.

Paragraph 190 (now paragraph 191) read, amended and agreed to.

Paragraphs 191 to 197 (now paragraphs 192 to 198) read and agreed to.

Paragraph 198 (now paragraph 199) read, amended and agreed to.

Paragraphs 199 to 202 (now paragraphs 200 to 203) read and agreed to.

Paragraph 203 (now paragraph 204) read, amended and agreed to.

Paragraphs 204 to 208 (now paragraphs 205 to 209) read and agreed to.

Paragraph 209 (now paragraph 210) read, amended and agreed to.

Paragraphs 210 to 212 (now paragraphs 211 to 213) read and agreed to.

Paragraph 213 (now paragraph 214) read, amended and agreed to.

Paragraph 214 (now paragraph 215) read and agreed to.

Paragraph 215 (now paragraph 216) read, amended and agreed to.

Paragraphs 216 to 219 (now paragraphs 217 to 220) read and agreed to.

Paragraph 220 (now paragraph 221) read, amended and agreed to.

Paragraphs 221 and 222 (now paragraphs 222 and 223) read and agreed to.

Paragraphs 223 to 227 (now paragraphs 224 to 228) read and agreed to.

Paragraphs 228 and 229 (now paragraphs 229 and 230) read, amended and agreed to.

Paragraphs 230 to 234 (now paragraphs 231 to 235) read and agreed to.

Paragraph 235 (now paragraph 236) read, amended and agreed to.

Paragraph 236 (now paragraph 237) read and agreed to.

Paragraphs 237 to 239 (now paragraphs 238 to 240) read, amended and agreed to.

Paragraph 240 (now paragraph 241) read and agreed to.

Paragraph 241 (now paragraph 242) read, amended and agreed to.

Paragraphs 242 to 246 (now paragraphs 243 to 247) read and agreed to.

Paragraph 247 (now paragraph 248) read, amended and agreed to.

Paragraphs 248 to 253 (now paragraphs 249 to 254) read and agreed to.

Paragraphs 254 to 256 (now paragraphs 255 to 257) read, amended and agreed to.

Ordered, That further consideration of the Chairman's draft Report be now adjourned.—(*The Chairman.*)

Report to be further considered this day.

[Adjourned till this day at Four o'clock.

WEDNESDAY 23 JUNE 1993
[AFTERNOON SESSION]

Members present:

Mr David Howell, in the Chair

Mr Dennis Canavan	Mr Peter Shore
Mr Mike Gapes	Sir John Stanley
Mr Jim Lester	Mr David Sumberg
Mr Ted Rowlands	Mr Robert N Wareing

The Committee deliberated.

Consideration of the Chairman's draft Report resumed.

Paragraph 257 (now paragraph 258) read, amended and agreed to.

A paragraph—(*Mr Dennis Canavan.*)—brought up, read the first and second time, amended and inserted (now paragraph 259).

Paragraph 258 (now paragraph 260) read, amended and agreed to.

Paragraph 259 read as follows:

"Since the disintegration of the Cold War balance of power, demands for the United Nations to try to resolve conflict, or to relieve suffering or abuse, have dramatically increased and the United Nations' response has been to extend the number, type and scale of its operations. The outstanding success of the UN-authorised operation to reverse Iraq's act of aggression against Kuwait has been followed by new demands for the UN to take action in situations far more complex than the act of invasion by one country of a neighbouring state. In Cambodia about 16,000 troops wearing blue berets have been deployed together with very large numbers of civilian personnel; in Somalia the number is around 28,000. Over thirty countries have contributed personnel to each of those operations. The operation in former Yugoslavia has been extended from the original peacekeeping operation in Croatia and a narrowly defined humanitarian relief operation in Bosnia. It is conceivable that UN personnel will be deployed there in even greater numbers than in Cambodia or Somalia. In both Somalia and Bosnia humanitarian relief operations are becoming enforcement operations carried out by heavily armed international troops backed up by air power. It seems possible that the UN will be called upon to maintain its presence for a long time in both countries. At the same time as these massive interventions, there are nine other UN peacekeeping operations at the time we complete this Report, of which one, in Mozambique, is planned to involve 8,000 troops."

An Amendment made.

Another Amendment proposed, in line 3, to delete from the word "operations" to the word "has" in line 4 and to insert the words "The achievement of the UN-backed operation to remove Iraqi troops from Kuwait".—(*Mr Dennis Canavan.*)

Question put That the Amendment be made.

The Committee divided.

Ayes, 1	Noes, 4
Mr Dennis Canavan	Mr Ted Rowlands
	Sir John Stanley
	Mr David Sumberg
	Mr Robert N Wareing

Other Amendments made.

Paragraph (now paragraph 261), as amended, agreed to.

Paragraphs 260 and 261 (now paragraphs 262 and 263) read, amended and agreed to.

Paragraphs 262 to 264 (now paragraphs 264 to 266) read and agreed to.

Paragraph 265 (now paragraph 267) read, amended and agreed to.

Paragraphs 266 to 268 (now paragraphs 268 to 270) read and agreed to.

Postponed paragraph 1 read, amended and agreed to.

Annexes A to D read and agreed to.

Resolved, That the Report, as amended, be the Third Report of the Committee to the House.

Ordered, That the Chairman do make the Report to the House.

Ordered, That the provisions of Standing Order No 116 (Select Committees (reports)) be applied to the Report.

Several papers were ordered to be appended to the Minutes of Evidence.

Ordered, That the Appendices to the Minutes of Evidence taken before the Committee be reported to the House—(*The Chairman*.)

[Adjourned till Wednesday 7 July at Ten o'clock.

LIST OF WITNESSES

Wednesday 5 May 1993

FOREIGN AND COMMONWEALTH OFFICE

Rt Hon Douglas Hurd CBE MP, Mr Alan Charlton and Mr Paul Lever CMG   228

LIST OF MEMORANDA INCLUDED IN THE MINUTES OF EVIDENCE

LIST OF APPENDICES TO THE
MINUTES OF EVIDENCE

Printed in the United Kingdom for HMSO.
Dd.5060917, 7/93, C9, 3398/3, 5673, 248009.

ISBN 0-10-020713-8